This is an impressive work, certainly the most comprehensive, coherent treatment of the workplace smoking problem ever published anywhere. This book should be available in every office.

> Donald T. Wigle MD, PhD, MPH
> Chief
> Non-communicable Disease Division
> Laboratory Centre for Disease Control
> Health and Welfare Canada

Your book contains very useful and informative material and should be helpful to individuals establishing smoking policies in the workplace... your efforts are worth pursuing.

> C. Everett Koop MD
> Surgeon General
> United States Public Health Service

...packed with medical and legal information to help beleaguered non-smokers who now smoke involuntarily at work.

> Sidney Katz
> Author, Journalist, Broadcaster

Smoke in the workplace is a major environmental health issue in the 1980s. This book will go a long way toward giving non-smokers the facts they need in order to protect their health at work.

> Roger Cotton
> Past Chairman
> Canadian Environmental Law
>   Association

Second-hand smoke in the workplace is not just a nuisance. It's a proven occupational health hazard and this book shows why. Great work!

> J. David Stewart MD, DECH, CCFP
> Head, Department of Occupational
>   Health and Safety
> Sunnybrook Medical Centre
> University of Toronto

About the author…

Martin Dewey is a journalist with extensive experience in the print and electronic media. He was a staff writer with *The Globe and Mail* "Report on Business" and has served on the editorial boards of *The Toronto Star* and other Canadian newspapers. While with *The Toronto Star* he won a National Newspaper Award for his editorial writing.

He has been a writer and editor for both the CBC and CTV national television news programs.

ACKNOWLEDGEMENTS

The author gratefully acknowledges the comments and criticisms of all those who found time amid busy schedules to review the draft manuscript. For help with medical and scientific material, the author wishes to mention the special contribution of the following: Donald T. Wigle, M.D., and Neil E. Collishaw, of Health and Welfare Canada, as well as James Repace of the U.S. Environmental Protection Agency. For help with the legal sections, particular thanks are owing to Lewis Eisen, Brenda Cox-Graham, Roger Cotton, Paul Cotton and Allan Millard, as well as to David Lampert of the Canadian Centre for Occupational Health and Safety. Special thanks are also extended to Donna Shimp of Environmental Improvement Associates in Salem, New Jersey; Regina Carlson of New Jersey GASP; and Robert Rosner of Rosner, Weis and Lowenberg, Inc., Seattle, Wash. For research and typing, the author acknowledges the cheerful help of Chris Pryde and Sherry Gilad. A special debt of gratitude is owed to Garfield Mahood, executive director of the Non-Smokers' Rights Association, whose enthusiasm and expertise were of inestimable value to the writing project. Finally, the author wishes to thank old friends of the NSRA whose moral support and unstinting generosity made it all possible.

VERY SPECIAL THANKS

The author and staff of the NSRA offer particular thanks to Gord Krull, President, Bob Kirilenko, Jerry Chalmers, Ted Fullerton and their associates on the staff of Qualitype Company of Toronto, for their generosity and, above all, their patience.

Smoke in the Workplace

AN ACTION MANUAL
FOR NON-SMOKERS

by

MARTIN DEWEY

NON-SMOKERS' RIGHTS ASSOCIATION
SMOKING AND HEALTH ACTION FOUNDATION

NC PRESS LIMITED
TORONTO 1986

We would like to thank the Ontario Arts Council and the Canada Council for their assistance in the production of this book.

Canadian Cataloguing in Publication Data

Dewey, Martin.
  Smoke in the workplace

Includes bibliographical references.
ISBN 0-920053-75-0

1. Smoking – Prevention – Handbooks, manuals, etc.
2. Work environment. I. Non-Smokers' Rights Association.
II. Title.

HV5733.D49 1986   363.1'9   C86-093647-3

New Canada Publications, a division of NC Press Limited
Box 4010, Station A, Toronto, Ontario, Canada M5H 1H8

Printed and bound in Canada.

Distributed in the United States of America by
Independent Publishers Group, One Pleasant Avenue, Port Washington, New York 11050

Contents

JAN 1988

Smoke in the Workplace

THINGS YOU SHOULD KNOW:

- Second-hand smoke used to be considered just a nuisance. It is now known to be a cause of disease and even premature death in nonsmokers.

- Smoke that hangs in the indoor air contains more than 50 known carcinogens, or cancer-causing substances.

- Building ventilation systems don't eliminate tobacco-generated contamination from the air – they spread it around.

- So-called "light" cigarettes actually increase indoor air pollution.

- Segregating smoking and nonsmoking employees adds to the health risk for nonsmokers.

- Employees have both a moral and a legal right to a smoke-free workplace.

- A smoke-free workplace has been shown to benefit everyone – nonsmokers, smokers and employers.

1

annoying

NOT JUST A NUISANCE

"No longer is smoking simply a 'nuisance' to nonsmokers. Today the evidence proves the effects of second-hand or involuntary smoking are severe enough to make smoking everyone's concern."
— Ontario Medical Association. [1]

Beginning with a startling series of medical findings in Britain and the United States in the 1960s, the world has been left in no doubt that **active** smoking is a cause of disease and early death. In Canada alone, government estimates indicate that more than 550 smokers die from smoking-related diseases every week. [2]

More recently, however, international studies have found that it is not just active smokers who are harmed. Health damage is suffered by all who share indoor space with smokers — and the greatest damage of all is suffered by nonsmoking fellow workers.

Surveys show that few nonsmokers are indifferent to second-hand smoke. In some, the reaction is mere annoyance. In others it produces physical irritation. In still others it produces disease and, yes, even death.

Annoyance...
- A U.S. survey found that more than 60 per cent of respondents — and they included smokers as well as nonsmokers — agreed with the statement: "It is annoying to be near a person who is smoking cigarettes." [3]

- A study of nonsmoking government workers in Baltimore, Md., found that more than half felt their productivity was impaired by second-hand smoke and 14 per cent found it difficult to produce work. [4]

- A survey covering more than 1,000 Canadians and published in the *Canadian Journal of Public Health* reported that 52.5% were annoyed by smoking in offices, with 26 per cent complaining of "major" annoyance — and nearly half the sample were smokers. [5]

Physical Irritation...
- The same Canadian survey showed that more than eight out of 10

respondents experienced physical discomfort in the presence of second-hand smoke.

- According to James Repace, a scientist with the U.S. Environmental Protection Agency and a leading international authority on indoor air pollution: "Several studies have indicated that from one-half to three-fourths of nonsmoking adults experience symptomatic effects from ambient tobacco smoke exposure, including eye, nose, and throat irritation, headache and nausea, with much more severe effects reported in persons with cardiac or obstructive pulmonary disease." [6]

...Disease and Death

- An electrifying report in the *British Medical Journal* found in Japan that nonsmoking wives of heavy smokers develop lung cancer at nearly twice the rate of those whose husbands are nonsmokers. [7]

- A smaller study of nonsmoking wives in Greece found that the lung cancer risk to those married to smokers is twice to three times the risk run by those married to nonsmokers. [8]

- A study of 1,338 lung cancer patients in Louisiana found that non-smokers married to heavy smokers run an increased risk of cancer, and so do nonsmokers whose mothers smoked. [9]

- A U.S. study found that nonsmokers married to smokers had 60 per cent more cancers of all types than nonsmokers never married to smokers. [10]

- The U.S. Environmental Protection Agency estimates that second-hand smoke is to blame for up to 5,000 lung cancer deaths among nonsmoking Americans every year. [11]

- A 10-year study involving 2,100 San Diego office workers found a "significant" impairment of small airways function among nonsmokers who had worked 20 years or more in enclosed areas where smoking was permitted. **They were found to have the same level of impairment as people who smoke up to 10 cigarettes a day.** [12]

- A French study of 8,000 adults found that nonsmokers 40 years of age and older who were married to smokers had impaired lung function which could be explained only by exposure to second-hand smoke in the home. [13]

- Other studies have found that children of smokers have higher-than-average rates of respiratory impairment and disease. It has also been shown that sudden infant death syndrome is more prevalent in smoking households. [14]

- A recent U.S. study calculates that 10,000 to 50,000 American non-smokers actually die every year as a result of long-term exposure to relatively low levels of second-hand smoke. [15]

Since Canadians tend to smoke more heavily than Americans, as we will show, the death rates among nonsmokers in this country will be proportionately higher. It should be noted, moreover, that these studies report the effects of second-hand tobacco smoke on otherwise healthy people. But large numbers of Canadians are particularly vulnerable to the contaminants in second-hand smoke owing to pre-existing health problems such as heart disease, acute respiratory disease, bronchitis, emphysema, asthma and hay fever. According to Health and Welfare Canada, one in five Canadians is in this special risk situation. [16]

CONFIRMATION IN THE LABS

Epidemiological findings are buttressed by a wealth of studies on test animals in which the effects of exposure to second-hand smoke are measured in controlled settings. Here are some results: [17]

- A "significant" number of mice exposed to second-hand smoke over one or two years developed severe bronchitis and inflammation of the bronchial tubes.

- Rabbits exposed to smoke from 20 cigarettes a day for two to five years developed emphysema (destruction of the air sacs in the lungs).

- Dogs exposed to cigarette smoke 10 times a week for one year suffered a breakdown of lung tissues.

- Rats exposed to second-hand smoke for 45 minutes a day for two to six months developed twice as many lung tumors as a control group.

Health problems developed in some test animals after exposure to as few as four cigarettes a day. One research team exposed 200 mice to cigarette smoke for only 20 minutes a day, every other day. Eight of the mice developed cancerous growths, while none did in a non-exposed control group. [18] **It should be noted that these exposures were much lower than those experienced by nonsmokers in typical workplace conditions.**

How valid are animal tests in predicting human reactions to second-hand smoke? Spokesmen for the tobacco industry contend that the findings are irrelevant. They say we can't automatically assume that animals and humans will react in the same way, and that animal tests may involve exaggerated exposures to disease-causing substances. In fact, however, animal tests are a standard prerequisite to obtaining governmental approval for new drugs and food substances. If we accept that such tests can tell us when a product is safe, we must also accept that they can tell when a product isn't safe.

"I don't know of any serious, independent scientist," observes Dr. Samuel Epstein, author of *The Politics of Cancer,* "who challenges the predictive evidence of animal tests. Virtually every major chemical carcinogen which has been recognized in humans was first identified in animals." [19]

11

2

THE GREAT HEALTH DEBATE

> "The public apparently has great concern for acid rain and other environmental pollution problems... In contrast, the majority of nonsmokers seem blissfully unaware of the health hazards due to their exposure to tobacco smoke."
> – D. T. Wigle, Chief, Non-Communicable Disease Division,
> Laboratory Centre for Disease Control,
> Health and Welfare Canada. [20]

If it can be shown that second-hand smoke causes disease and death in nonsmokers, why hasn't there been an outcry? Why are nonsmokers still putting up with it?

The answer is that the message hasn't been getting through – and it's no accident. Medical warnings have to contend with a massive and continuing effort by the world-wide tobacco industry to portray smoking as a benign activity that does no harm to anyone, smoker or nonsmoker. A second line of product-defence is for the industry to challenge what it takes to be adverse medical findings, or to fund researchers of its own who can be relied upon to do the challenging. A favorite theme is that no one has yet found the "smoking gun" – that is, a specific disease-causing mechanism in tobacco.

"Can We Have an Open Debate About Smoking?" asks a full-page magazine ad paid for by the R. J. Reynolds Tobacco Co. "Over the years you've heard so many negative reports about smoking and health – and so little to challenge these reports – that you may assume the case against smoking is closed. But this is far from the truth. Studies which conclude that smoking causes disease have regularly ignored scientific evidence to the contrary. These scientific findings come from research completely independent of the tobacco industry. We at R. J. Reynolds think you will find such evidence very interesting. Because we think reasonable people who analyze it may come to see this issue not as a closed case, but as an open controversy." [21]

The call for an open debate will come as something of a surprise to journalists, health agencies and nonsmokers' rights groups which have found it virtually impossible to persuade tobacco industry personnel to take part in public exchanges of any kind. But the real clanger in the advertisement is the statement that there has been "so little" to challenge the medical evidence. The fact is that challenging the evidence – by portraying smoking as a happy, healthy activity – is one of the main reasons that tobacco advertising budgets have reached stratospheric heights.

THE ROLE OF ADVERTISING

"Every year," writes Peter Taylor in his book *The Smoke Ring*, "the tobacco industry spends around $2 billion globally to ensure that cigarettes are associated with glamor, success and sophistication, instead of lung cancer, bronchitis and heart disease. The industry needs to make this huge and ever-increasing investment to perpetuate this false image in order to counter the evidence that cigarettes are not desirable but dangerous. After addiction, advertising is the industry's most powerful ally in its battle for the hearts and minds of the smoker and in its drive to seduce more recruits into the Smoke Ring." [22]

A similar observation was made in a confidential study of tobacco advertising carried out by the U.S. Federal Trade Commission. "The dominant themes of cigarette advertising," said the investigators, "are that smoking is associated with youthful vigor, good health, good looks and personal, social and professional acceptance and success, and that it is compatible with a wide range of athletic and healthful activities." [23]

A Successful Strategy

Tragically, the strategy works. Here is what FTC researchers found after examining a number of opinion polls and commissioning two of their own:

"It has been almost 17 years since the [U.S.] Surgeon-General first determined that cigarette smoking is hazardous to health," they wrote. "For 15 years, warnings to that effect have appeared on cigarette packages and, for almost 10 years, warnings have also appeared on every cigarette ad.

"Yet survey data indicate that a substantial portion of people remain unaware of the serious overall health risk associated with smoking. The data, projected nationwide, indicate that some Americans still do not even know that smoking is hazardous to health."

The surveys indicated that up to 17 per cent of smokers, or up to 10 million smoking individuals, didn't know that there are any health hazards at all. Fully 41 per cent, or 20 million smokers, didn't know about reduced life expectancy. Half, or 25 million smokers, didn't know that smoking is responsible for almost all lung cancers. And so it went, question after question. [24]

THE CASE IS CLOSED

Although the tobacco industry appears to have confused large sections of the public on the health question, there is no confusion whatever in the medical and scientific community. While it's always possible to argue over the technical details of studies, researchers are not divided on the underlying issue. Never in the history of disease has a subject been so intensively researched. Never in the history of medicine has the cause of an epidemic been demonstrated with such certainty.

> "The success story of medical research over the last 30 years has been the production of unassailable evidence that cigarette smoking is the cause of the 20th century epidemic of lung cancer."
> – British epidemiologist Michael Coleman. [25]

Says the Canadian Medical Association in an unusually forthright utterance: "The story of the health hazards created by cigarette smoking represents an unrivalled tale of illness, disability and death. The potential benefits to be derived from the cessation of smoking place it at a level of importance in preventive medicine with pasteurization of milk, the purification and chlorination of water, and immunization." [26]

And here is Britain's Royal College of Physicians on the subject: "Action to protect the public against the damage done to so many of them by cigarette smoking would have more effect upon the public health in this country than anything else that can now be done in the whole field of preventive medicine." [27]

Smoking has also been condemned in a series of reports by the U.S. surgeon general. In the 1983 report, tobacco products are blamed for 3 million deaths from heart disease between 1965 and 1980 in the U.S. alone. Unless smoking habits change, the report says, tobacco-caused coronary heart disease may kill "10 percent of all persons now alive... The total number of such deaths may exceed 24 million." [28]

The 1982 surgeon general's report says that 30 per cent of **all** cancer deaths are caused by smoking, and that "cigarette smoking is the major single cause of cancers of the lung, larynx, oral cavity and esophagus, and is a contributory factor for the development of cancers of the bladder, pancreas and kidney." [29]

The tone of these statements does not suggest the health question is still "open." The medical and scientific community has been telling us for years that active smoking kills and disables, and now it is saying the same thing about exposure to second-hand smoke.

While it's true that no one has yet found the famous smoking gun, this in no way weakens the case. The clear statistical correlation between a list of medical conditions on the one hand, and exposure to tobacco smoke on the other, leaves medical researchers in no doubt about the cause.

"If we apply the same standard of proof that says we have not yet proven that smoking causes lung cancer," observes William Weis, a professor at Seattle University and a leading expert on smoking pollution in the workplace, "then neither have we proven that viruses cause the common cold, that bacteria cause strept throat or, in a slightly different vein, that smallpox vaccinations had even the slightest preventive influence on that once-dreaded disease." [30]

Self-Serving Research

A final word about industry-funded health research. In pointing to various sums spent in laboratories, the tobacco companies would like us to believe that they are as interested in the health question as anyone else. But the research has been overwhelmingly self-interested, concentrating mainly on the search for a "safe" cigarette. It's hoped that the toxic properties in tobacco can be identified and removed so that smoking can be restored to full social acceptability.

This is a bizarre hope, considering that making a safe cigarette would involve removing the very substances that make people smoke in the first place. And, sure enough, the search for a safe cigarette has proved to be a waste of money. In the meantime the toll of disease and death continues, and the cigarette makers continue to spend billions on advertising every year to ensure that it does.

> *"Every year cigarettes kill more Americans than were killed in World War I, the Korean war and Vietnam combined; nearly as many as died in World War II. Each year cigarettes kill five times more Americans than do traffic accidents. Lung cancer alone kills as many as die on the road. THE CIGARETTE INDUSTRY IS PEDDLING A DEADLY WEAPON. IT IS DEALING IN PEOPLE'S LIVES FOR FINANCIAL GAIN."* – The late U.S. Senator Robert Kennedy. [31]

3

A NATION OF SMOKERS

> "Although the proportion of smokers has declined...the daily PER CAPITA consumption by smokers has risen...Our indoor atmosphere is getting smokier every year."
> – Dr. Peter Morgan, Scientific Editor,
> Canadian Medical Association Journal. [32]

Among Canada's many distinctions, there is one we can't be too proud of. It's that our indoor air is more polluted, more hazardous to lungs and health, than that of most other countries in the world. The reason is that Canadians smoke more than most other people. Consider the following statistics for 1983:

- In a 131-nation survey, Canada tied with the United States and Japan for fourth place in per capita consumption of manufactured cigarettes – just behind Cyprus, Cuba and Greece. [33]

- Canadians smoked 10 times more roll-your-own cigarettes than Americans did. High sales of these unfiltered, high-tar and high-nicotine cigarettes placed Canada well ahead of the United States in over-all per capita cigarette consumption. [34]

- In the over-20 age bracket, 35 to 36 per cent of Canadians were regular smokers, compared to only 32 per cent in the United States. [35]

- Canadians puffed their way through more than 70 billion cigarettes. That was 192 million cigarettes a day, or 8 million cigarettes an hour around the clock! [36]

That Canadians continue to smoke so much is a tragedy. But it doesn't end there, for smokers routinely choose to smoke in ways that impose the consequences on those around them. Although the average cigarette burns for 12 minutes, the smoker puffs on it for only about 24 seconds. [37]

Thus only a small fraction of the smoke produced by the cigarette is directly inhaled by the smoker; most of it is discharged into the surrounding air to be inhaled by others. Heavy smokers repeat this performance several times an hour, and even average smokers will light up between 1.5 and 2 times an hour. These patterns ensure that new smoke will be added to the air before smoke from previous cigarettes has dissipated. [38]

WHEN SOME SMOKE, EVERYONE SMOKES

It would be hard to devise a more unfortunate way of delivering a chemical to the brain. When someone downs a drink, the liquid passes through the mouth and into the drinker's system. When an addict takes heroin, the drug is fed directly into the user's veins. But when someone lights a cigarette indoors, the drug is delivered to everyone present. Because of this, it is misleading to discuss the health consequences of tobacco addiction in terms of smokers and nonsmokers. In a very real sense, virtually all Canadians are smokers. Here are some recent findings:

- Fully 85 per cent of urban adults are forced to breathe other people's smoke on a daily basis, with the average nonsmoking adult inhaling 1.4 mg of tobacco tar a day. [39]

- "Virtually all urban nonsmokers have measurable amounts of nicotine in their body fluids throughout most of their lives," says a report in *Lancet,* the prestigious British medical journal. "It is derived from the indoor air they breathe and it requires no more than one or two smokers to contaminate a vehicle or a building." [40]

- Scientists at Kyoto University in Japan examined levels of cotinine (a byproduct of nicotine) in the urine of nonsmokers. The levels were three times higher among nonsmokers who work with smokers than among those working in a smoke-free environment. "We conclude," they write, "that the deleterious effects of passive smoking may occur in proportion to the exposure of nonsmokers in the home, the workplace and the community...Smokers ought to be discouraged from smoking when working in the same room with nonsmokers." [41]

- Tests have recorded significant carbon monoxide levels in the blood of nonsmokers after as little as half an hour in the company of smokers. [42]

- In a Dutch study, eight nonsmokers had carcinogens in their urine after spending six hours with heavy smokers in a poorly ventilated room. [43]

4

THE WORKPLACE AS SMOKE TRAP

At first glance, the workplace is where nonsmokers would be least likely to suffer health damage from second-hand smoke. Unlike our homes, which usually rely on random ventilation, the places in which we work are frequently equipped with complex ventilation systems. Designers of modern buildings speak glowingly of "computerized climate control," of "filtered air" and of three, four and five "complete air changes" per hour. In addition, the lawbooks are heavy with regulations designed to ensure that employers provide safe and healthy working conditions. Where the workplace is concerned, it would seem that indoor man has truly made up for God's outdoor deficiencies.

The reality, however, is that one pollutant – tobacco smoke – has managed to beat the system. According to Repace: "The smoke pollution inhaled indirectly from cigarettes, pipes and cigars indoors is not only chemically related to the smoke from factory chimneys, but routinely occurs at far higher levels indoors than does factory smoke or automobile exhaust outdoors...Substantial air pollution burdens are inflicted upon nonsmokers far in excess of those encountered in smoke-free indoor environments, outdoors, or in vehicles on busy commuter highways." [44]

Repace and a co-researcher, Alfred Lowrey of the U.S. Naval Research Laboratory, have calculated average exposures to second-hand smoke in the home and at work. "Our estimates show," they write, "that the ratio of workplace dose to the exposure received at home is nearly four to one – indicating that, on average, the workplace is a more important source of exposure than the home environment." They conclude that a nonsmoker in an office with typical ventilation and a typical population of smokers inhales the equivalent of three low-tar cigarettes in an eight-hour day. [45] But if the office is poorly ventilated – which, as we will see, is more common than you may think – nonsmokers may inhale the equivalent of 10 cigarettes in their working day, and possibly more! [46]

In other words the workplace, which **should** be a refuge from tobacco smoke, is the place of greatest exposure for nonsmokers. It also tends to be the place of **longest** exposure. Substances that have been shown to attack the respiratory systems of test animals after mere hours of exposure may be absorbed by the nonsmoker as a matter of daily routine throughout his or her working life. Worse, the workplace is where nonsmokers tend to have least control over their surroundings. We can choose whether to put up with second-hand smoke in many situations, but most of us have to go to work and accept the conditions we find there. The workplace is where the term "forced smoking" all too often has literal meaning; it is where the need to attack the second-hand smoke problem is most urgent, and where the potential gains for the nonsmoker are greatest.

THE VENTILATION PROBLEM

To understand how tobacco smoke beats the system, we must take a closer look at its chemical composition. An exceedingly fine aerosol, it contains at least 3,800 identified compounds and occurs in two phases – gases and airborne particles. The gas phase contains such poisons and irritants as carbon monoxide, formaldehyde, acrolein, ammonia, nitrogen oxides, pyridine and hydrogen cyanide. It also contains 16 known or probable cancer-causing agents. [47] One of these is N-nitrosodimethylamine – or NDMA – which, according to the International Agency for Research on Cancer, "produces cancer in all animal species in which it has been tested and does so by various exposure routes, including inhalation, and after single doses." [48]

The particulate phase contains tars and nicotine (itself a powerful poison) as well as 38 known or probable carcinogens. [49] Among them are 2-naphthylamine and 4-aminobiphenyl. According to guidelines published by the American Conference of Governmental Industrial Hygienists, there is no safe exposure level for these two substances: "No exposure or contact by any route – respiratory, skin or oral, as detected by the most sensitive methods – shall be permitted." [50]

Mainstream, Sidestream

Ironically, ambient smoke inhaled by nonsmokers is in some respects chemically more dangerous than smoke inhaled directly by smokers. Directly inhaled smoke – referred to as mainstream smoke – loses some of its toxicity on the way to the lungs. Some contaminants are burned off in the higher temperatures produced by puffing, and the smoke is twice-filtered as it passes through unburned tobacco and then through the filter itself. Smoke which rises from the burning end of an idling cigarette – called sidestream smoke – is produced at lower temperatures, which means more of the contaminants remain intact, and it enters the environment without being filtered in any way. Compared with smoke inhaled directly, sidestream smoke breathed by the nonsmoker contains twice the nicotine, twice the tar, three times the pyrene and phenols, three times the ben-zopyrene and five times the carbon monoxide. [51] It also contains 50 times more of the carcinogen NDMA. [52] (If there seems to be an incon-sistency here – after all, nonsmokers still have a lower mortality rate than smokers – we have to remember that smokers inhale both sidestream and mainstream smoke.)

Filters That Don't Filter

Although building engineers talk of air changes per hour, or ACH, the air is not changed so much as it is recycled. It is drawn out of an indoor space, passed through filters, and then returned. It's the same air as before, the only difference being that standard ventilation specifications call for adding 10 per cent new outdoor air to the flow.

Even this rudimentary recycling would help if the air were properly cleaned. Unfortunately, most buildings are equipped with low-efficiency mechanical filters that do little to control airborne contaminants. Although there are high-efficiency filters that remove many pollutants from the air, they are expensive to install and maintain, and tend to be used only in special circumstances where air purity is deemed to be of overriding importance.

"It's really a cost situation," says Herbert Maybank, a Toronto consulting engineer and filtration specialist. "Building designers won't make ventilation systems any better than they have to. When a construction project goes over budget, almost without exception it is filter quality that will be cut. The value of filters is generally not perceived." [53]

A Mini-World

The first drawback of mechanical filters, even the good ones, is that they are not designed to remove gases from the air. Since some of the most dangerous constituents of tobacco smoke are found in its gaseous phase, this has to be considered a fatal drawback.

What about the airborne particulates in second-hand smoke, with their 38 known or probable carcinogens? To understand this aspect of the ventilation problem we must enter the mini-world of particles, which range in size from visible specks all the way down to particles so fine that they can be detected only by an electron microscope or an optical counter. The unit of measurement is the micron, with 25,400 microns to the inch. The dot on this "i" might be 400 microns, while a human hair might be 40 microns and pollen might go down to 10 microns.

To start with, the cheap filters installed in most low-cost buildings have almost no effect on smaller airborne particles. As Maybank jokingly expresses it: "They are only good for trapping moths, flies and rocks." But even good mechanical filters found in well-equipped buildings rapidly lose efficiency below one micron. And this is the second fatal drawback of building filtration systems, for most of the particles in tobacco smoke are smaller than one micron. Like the gases, they pass right through the filters. [54]

If filters in ventilation systems don't remove the tobacco-generated gases from the air, and let 99 percent of the particles pass through, what good are they? [55] The question answers itself. The fact is, **air filters leave off where tobacco smoke begins.**

Not-So-Fresh Air

Since filters have little effect on the problem, the only way ventilation systems can reduce the level of second-hand smoke in the workplace is by diluting it with fresh air from outdoors. But this air must be heated in winter and cooled in summer, so once again we encounter a situation in which cost considerations militate against indoor air quality. With no government regulations to force building operators to adhere to design specifications, they may be tempted to reduce the fresh air intake for reasons of economy or, if they prefer, energy conservation. Repace has come across U.S. government buildings where there was no fresh air at all. As he says, "The lack of enforcement of design ventilation rates is a serious problem." [56]

We've seen that even a conscientiously operated ventilation system provides only about 10 per cent fresh air, which means the dilution process is a very slow one. Repace has shown that in a work area ventilated at the rate of one air change an hour, it takes more than three hours to get rid of the smoke from a single cigarette. Even at three air changes an hour it takes an hour to get rid of most of the smoke. The catch is that the average smoker goes through 1.5 to two cigarettes an hour. With a single smoker in a room, smoke from Cigarette Two will be added to the atmosphere while the system is still laboring with the smoke from Cigarette One. Usually, of course, there will be more than one smoker in an indoor space – which means that the ventilation system will fall behind all the faster.

Writes Repace: **"Under the practical range of ventilation conditions and building occupation densities, the respirable particle levels generated by smokers under typical conditions overwhelm the effects of ventilation even when applicable standards are observed."** [57]

Needed: A Small Gale

> *"Recent studies of ventilation requirements for tobacco smoke indicate that SMOKING INDOORS IS TOTALLY INCOMPATIBLE WITH GOOD HEALTH AND CLEAN INDOOR AIR. Tobacco smoke is just too efficient a pollution source to ventilate properly without large expenditures on equipment and energy."*
> – Indoor Air Pollution and Housing Technology:
>   1983 report to Canada Mortgage and Housing Corporation.

According to Repace, a nonsmoker who finds himself in a typical workplace situation with standard ventilation and an average distribution of smokers can expect to inhale a level of nicotine, tars and other toxic substances equivalent to between two and three cigarettes every single working day. [58] Over a working lifetime of 40 years, he says, a nonsmoker's risk of lung cancer is "250 times the maximum lifetime value considered acceptable." [59]

What would be required in such a workplace to reduce the health risk to nonsmokers to an "acceptable" level? To find out, Repace and Lowrey developed an experimental model. Calculating for only one cigarette-induced disease, lung cancer, they assumed that an acceptable level of risk would be one case per 100,000 nonsmokers over a 40-year work life. This, they point out, is the value considered acceptable under "commonly used environmental criteria for carcinogenic contaminants in air, water or food." In order to reduce the lung cancer risk to nonsmokers to this level, they found, an indoor work area with a typical mix of smokers and nonsmokers would require 226 air changes an hour! In other words, a small gale. [60]

BEWARE THE 'CLEAN BILL OF HEALTH'

We have seen that building ventilation systems are simply not designed to protect employees from the contaminants in second-hand smoke. It's the same with government air safety regulations in the workplace. When they were drafted, lawmakers were mainly concerned with protecting smelter workers, garage mechanics, factory hands and such workers from the heavy concentrations of pollutants that can be encountered in industrial settings. Tobacco smoke was not thought of as a pollutant.

This is why a government air safety inspector can walk into a workplace that is polluted with tobacco smoke and give it a clean bill of health. The fact is, he will have used a set of tests designed to detect industrial pollutants and will not have tested for tobacco smoke *per se*. As we pointed out, the 3,800 substances contained in tobacco smoke come in the form of gases and airborne particulates. Government air tests measure only a few selected gases such as carbon dioxide, carbon monoxide, formaldehyde and nitrogen oxides. The airborne **particles** in tobacco smoke are not measured at all.

"The big thing to measure for," according to Repace, "is the level of respirable particles. There are 60 carcinogens in tobacco smoke and 50 are found in the particulate phase. Any test that doesn't look for respirable particles is a red herring." [61]

Moreover, the guidelines against which workplace air tests are measured were designed for industrial settings – not for ordinary workplaces. The guidelines are too broad to offer any protection against the contaminants in tobacco smoke – even the most lethal ones. In the case of carbon monoxide, the guidelines would be exceeded only in an extremely smoky setting such as a small, crowded conference room or a bar. Yet it has been established that even low levels of carbon monoxide – the kind you can encounter in any office where smokers are present – can cause head-aches, yawning, dizziness and nausea [62] as well as chest pains for those with angina pectoris. [63]

Other problems may arise from imprecise testing procedures. "The air concentrations of carbon monoxide and other contaminants from tobacco smoke are often measured at some distance from the nearest smoker and thus tend to be lower than those to which persons working close to smokers are exposed." So says a Health and Welfare Canada report, citing a finding by the U.S. surgeon-general. [64]

Finding the Killers

It is, in fact, possible to design effective air tests for the workplace. Repace bases a great deal of his research on an instrument called a piezobalance. This is a portable device, about the size of a fishing tackle box, which measures the level of respirable particles in the air.

The procedure is to take a reading in a workplace on a Monday morning, say, before the arrival of any personnel. A second reading, taken at the end of the day, will indicate the weight of respirable particles that have been added to the air by burning tobacco. Since these particles are known to contain a range of carcinogens, the health risk to nonsmokers can be readily demonstrated.

An even more precise demonstration can be provided if an air test is designed to measure specific tobacco contaminants. These can be selected by referring to the air quality guidelines published by the American Conference of Governmental Industrial Hygienists (ACGIH) and which are accepted as the North American workplace standard. The guidelines set out threshold limit values (TLVs) for airborne substances, indicating highest permissible levels.

Among the many toxic particulates in tobacco smoke, two stand out in the ACGIH listing: 2-Naphthylamine and 4-Aminobiphenyl. Both are known to be carcinogens and the TLV assigned to each of them in the guidelines is Zero. In other words, no exposure of any kind is to be permitted.

Among the many dangerous gases in tobacco smoke, one stands out in the listing: N-Nitrosodimethylamine (NDMA), also known as Dimethyl-nitrosamine. As we pointed out earlier, this is one of the most potent carcinogens known, and it has produced cancer in all animal species on which it has been tested, even after single doses. The ACGIH guidelines recommend avoiding exposure. [65]

By collecting particulate matter from workplace air that has been contaminated by tobacco smoke, scientists can verify the presence of 2-Naphthylamine and 4-Aminobiphenyl. Although these substances appear only in trace quantities, it must be remembered that ACGIH guidelines call for no exposure whatever and that there is indeed no "safe" level of exposure where potent carcinogens are concerned. NDMA, the third target substance, can be verified in a separate test of gases collected in the workplace.

At the very least, then, air tests based on a complaint about tobacco smoke should measure the particulate levels before and after smoking. At best, tests should seek to identify the presence of specific carcinogens. Although the latter tests can cost anywhere from $500 to $1,000 and possibly more, they could prove to be money well spent for an employer, a union or an employees' group that was seriously concerned about indoor air pollution. Scientific evidence that highly carcinogenic substances were in the air in measurable quantities would become a powerful argument – we would say an **unanswerable** argument – for doing something about it.

HALF-MEASURES AND NON-SOLUTIONS

The most direct, efficient and inexpensive way to control tobacco-generated pollution of workplace air is to control the source – that is, to prohibit smoking on the premises. But many employers are reluctant to take this obvious step. If standard ventilation doesn't do the trick then surely, they think, there must be some other way to eliminate the health risk to nonsmokers without upsetting smokers. Unfortunately, as this section will show, there isn't.

Segregation

Segregating smokers and nonsmokers is frequently the first thing that comes to mind when people decide "something should be done" about second-hand smoke. But we have already seen what is wrong with this solution. Although physical separation will spare nonsmokers the acute discomfort of a direct blast from a smoker's cigarette – and perhaps we should be thankful for small mercies – the nonsmoker remains exposed to smoke clouds drifting on air currents, to smoke that has become generally dispersed in the area, and to the contaminants being circulated by the ventilation system.

Far from being a remedy, segregation in the workplace may well increase the health risk to nonsmokers. The farther away nonsmokers are from the source of the smoke, the more likely they are to put up with it, and to suffer the health consequences day after day, year after year. The smoker who sits beside you and blows the contaminants in your face may actually be doing you a favor. You won't forget that the problem is there.

Smoking Lounges

Another frequently heard suggestion is that smoking be limited to "designated areas" such as smoking lounges. This is a more attractive proposition than others considered so far, but it has serious shortcomings. One is that employers quickly come to resent seeing people leave their working areas to smoke. Another is that such lounges are usually tied into the building's ventilation system. Thus all the smoke generated in the lounge finds its way into the general air supply, which is then recirculated just as if it had been generated in work areas.

If lounges are to be considered as a solution, they must be self-enclosed and equipped with separate ventilation. This can be done without great cost, for all it takes is an exhaust fan and a duct leading either to the outdoors or, building codes permitting, to a washroom ventilation system.

Air Cleaners and Ionizers

It's sometimes suggested that the problem can be eliminated at one swoop by installing special room air cleaners or handing out individual ion generators for desktops and work stations. Here is the view of Dr. Elaine Panitz, a U.S. specialist in occupational and environmental medicine:

"Various air cleaners have been proposed to cope with smoke indoors. An electrostatic precipitator removes droplets and particles (.01 to 0.40

24

microns in size) from air with high efficiency. Since some of the gases of smoke stick to the droplets and particles, these are removed by the electrostatic precipitator also. Unfortunately, more than 90 per cent of tobacco smoke is made up of gas molecules that are so tiny (.0002 to .01 microns) they cannot be removed by electrostatic precipitation. Equally ineffective are ion generators, which purport to remove particles, but not gas molecules, from air." [66]

Returning to Repace – he is, after all, a leading world expert on smoking and ventilation – we find that it would cost around $2,000 to install a room air cleaner capable of providing just over six air changes an hour. As we've seen, however, this rate of change would soon be overwhelmed by a typical distribution of smokers. To provide a level of ventilation required to reduce the nonsmoker's cancer risk to a level considered acceptable for other environmental pollutants would cost something like $30,000 **per smoker**. [67]

Repace also carried out experiments with ion generators, observing that "several manufacturers have been marketing several types of units which claim to 'remove' cigarette smoke, pollens, pet danders, house dust and other pollutants and irritants from the air. On the basis of these claims, such devices are being installed without any factual knowledge as to their actual effectiveness in removing air particulates...

"Such devices are usually quantitatively demonstrated by turning the unit on in a smoke-filled table-top aquarium. The smoke will disappear in very short order. While such a demonstration may be eye-catching, it is a totally useless measure of actual performance, as persons live neither in glass houses or in air volumes considerably less than one cubic meter in volume.

"It should be emphasized," Repace concludes, "that ionizers may be ineffective in removing gas-phase pollutants from indoor combustion, and thus should not be considered as substitutes for ventilation or source control" – that is, control of smoking. [68] "Moreover," he adds, "ionizers may affect levels of hormones in the body and may even facilitate the deposition of particles in the lungs of nonsmokers." [69]

The 'Light Cigarette' Myth

Some smokers think they cause less harm to themselves and those around them when they switch to so-called light cigarettes. Actually, the opposite is the case. A low-tar and low-nicotine rating on a cigarette does not mean it contains less of these substances. The cigarette just burns faster, providing fewer puffs and delivering lower levels of contaminants on that account. According to Canadian researchers, the sidestream emissions of light cigarettes actually contain one-third more total particulate matter than standard cigarettes. [70] Another problem is that smokers who switch to so-called light cigarettes tend to smoke more of them in order to maintain their accustomed nicotine dosage. [71] The result of the switch to light cigarettes is therefore more cigarettes, more smoke in the air, and more contaminants in the smoke.

5

COUNTING THE COSTS

An employer who is nervous about upsetting smokers may feel that the most expedient thing to do is to leave matters alone in hopes of maintaining the status quo. But such an employer should realize that the status quo is not neutral. Smoking on the job exerts a negative effect on the workplace: It is injurious to the health of employees, it leads to tensions and lowered employee morale, and it adds to the costs of doing business. We will look at these added costs in this section; the numbers will amaze you.

POLLUTION VS. PROFIT

> *"If industry does not accept any sort of obligation to control or change smoking behavior by restriction, health education or other persuasion, it should be able to recognize the cost it shoulders as a result of the habit – whether from sickness or less-organized symptomatic ill-health, from error and accident, fire [and] time wasted in smoking rituals..."*
> – James Athanasou, School of Public Health, University of Sydney, Australia. [72]

Smoking is a more expensive pastime than most Canadians realize. The costs are borne not just by smokers as they dig into their pockets at the cigarette counter but by society as a whole. A study for the Laboratory Centre for Disease Control, Health and Welfare Canada, estimates that Canada's dollar loss in 1979 due to tobacco-related death, disability and disease totalled $5.2 billion. [73] An earlier study in California estimated one year's loss due to smoking-related illness, property damage and absenteeism to be $1 billion in that state alone. [74]

Much of this continuing cost is shouldered directly by employers. According to Dr. Marvin Kristein, chief of the Health Economics Division, American Health Foundation, an average employee smoking a pack a day or more costs an employer about $624 a year (1980 U.S. dollars) in extra expenses due to higher insurance premiums of various kinds, lowered productivity (including that of nonsmoking co-workers), absenteeism, disability and premature death.

Among the direct losses, he writes, are those resulting from "time lost due to smoking rituals; extra cleanup costs; extra damage to equipment, furniture and fixtures." Other costs result from "inefficiency and errors based on the established literature as to the effects of higher carbon monoxide levels in smokers, eye irritation, measured lowered attentiveness, cognitive and exercise capacity functioning." [75]

Another authority puts the loss much higher. William Weis of Seattle University, referred to earlier, lists the **extra** costs to an employer of a smoker whose total payroll costs are $30,000 a year as follows:

absenteeism	$ 330
medical care	230
disability, early death	770
fire, industrial accidents	90
time spent on smoking rituals	2,710
property damage, depreciation	500
maintenance	500

To these costs he adds the losses created by the chronic exposure of nonsmoking employees to second-hand smoke, which he calculates to be $245 per nonsmoker. Since statistics indicate that each smoker in the workplace is likely to share space with two nonsmokers, each smoker thus becomes responsible for another $490 in costs to the employer.

Prof. Weis's conclusion: A smoker whose total payroll costs are $30,000 a year costs his or her employer an additional $5,620 [in 1981 U.S. dollars] compared with a nonsmoking employee earning the same. [76]

After listing the studies on which he bases his findings, he says: "Trying to satisfy the sceptic that all these studies are accurate is a battle best left unengaged. One fact remains unchallenged: No matter how it is measured, smoking is a terrible drain on our economic resources." [77]

The Message of the Balance Sheet

Even sceptics must pay heed to the experience of a company like Dow Chemical. Concerned about possible smoking-related operating costs, the company instructed its medical department to undertake an extensive 3½-year study covering 1,400 employees at its Midland location in Texas. Here are some of the findings:

- Smokers were absent 5.5 days more per year than nonsmokers, costing Dow $657,146.73 annually in excess wage costs alone. This didn't include extra health care costs.
- Smokers registered 17.4 disability days per year, compared with 9.7 days for nonsmokers.
- Compared with nonsmokers, smokers had twice the circulatory disease problems, three times more pneumonia, 41% more bronchitis and emphysema, and 76% more respiratory diseases of all types.
- For every two nonsmokers who died during the study period, seven smokers died. [78]

A study of absenteeism at the United States Steel Corp. found, among other things, that "employees who smoke have more work-loss days than those who have never smoked. In every age group, as the number of cigarettes per day in confirmed smokers increases, so also does sick absence. Male smokers of more than two packs per day have nearly twice as much absence as their nonsmoking associates; the heaviest women smokers of more than two packs per day miss more than twice as much time as their counterparts who do not smoke [79]

The fire department in Alexandria, Virginia, began hiring nonsmokers exclusively after discovering that every firefighter who retired with smoking-related disabilities was costing the city an extra $140,000 in retirement benefits. "Why should the taxpayers subsidize it?" asked the fire chief. [80]

An article in *Supervisory Management* reports a survey in which 119 out of 223 Seattle-based managers indicate that they choose nonsmokers over smokers when faced with equally qualified applicants. [81] Citing several companies that have created nonsmoking areas, *Business Week* predicts that "many other companies, prodded by court decisions and stepped-up campaigns by anti-smoking health groups, will be forced to face the issue, sooner rather than later." [82]

FIGHTING BACK

As employers become aware of the costs of smoking in the workplace, many are starting to do something about it. Seattle-based Radar Electric Inc. doesn't hire smokers. The company president, Warren McPherson, says he instituted the policy after a company survey showed smokers were less productive than nonsmokers.

Comments a report in the *Wall Street Journal:* "Employers who shun smokers usually echo Mr. McPherson's complaint...They argue that people use cigarettes as a break from work. So smoking a pack of cigarettes on the job could mean 20 breaks a day. Smoking-related illness can also cause high absenteeism, says the National Centre for Health Statistics, which estimates that sick smokers cost [U.S.] businesses $25.8 billion in lost productivity in 1980." [83]

One U.S. daily quotes the owner of a company employing 240 people as saying: "You'd have to be crazy to hire smokers. They have a 22% higher sick time than nonsmokers. We save a half-million dollars in health benefits each year." [84]

'No Smoking' Signs Go Up

"Refusing to hire smokers is the most dramatic among many actions being taken by employers today to discourage smoking and protect nonsmokers," says Regina Carlson, a New Jersey health advocate. "Other responses include separate smoking and nonsmoking sections, banning smoke anywhere on company premises, offering cessation programs and paying bonuses to nonsmoking employees... .

"It is not just little maverick companies that are acting on smoking now. Among the biggies: Bell Labs, Coors, IBM, Campbell Soup, [the states of] Connecticut, Hawaii, Kansas, New Jersey, Maine, Control Data Corp., Dow Chemical, McGraw-Hill, Merle Norman, British Columbia Ministry of Health, Johns-Manville, Rodale Press, Kansas Department of Health and Environment, the U.S. General Services Administration, and [United States] Departments of Defence, Health and Human Services, Labor, and Environmental Protection." [85]

A Lead from Government

Since 1980, 6,500 employees of the British Columbia Ministry of Health have been prohibited from smoking in general work areas. Unfortunately, some of the good is undone by permitting the practice in private offices, where smoke can still contaminate the common air supply.

With this partial exception, Canadian governments have been slow off the mark in protecting the health of their own nonsmoking employees. But that is beginning to change, and two government departments have shown commendable leadership on the issue.

First to move was the Auditor-General's department in Ottawa. When a survey showed that nearly three-quarters of its 550 employees wanted smoking restrictions, the department banned the practice in all work areas. Those who wish to smoke must go to separately ventilated lounge areas on each floor.

The Department of Regional Industrial Expansion (DRIE), with 2,000 employees, is in the same Ottawa building. The personnel department heard what was happening in the Auditor-General's department and carried out its own survey. When fully 80 per cent said Yes to smoking restrictions, DRIE adopted the same policy as its neighbor. Because smoking has been restricted to separately ventilated areas, nonsmoking employees in both departments can now go about their work without having to inhale a trace of tobacco smoke.

The Department of Health and Welfare, with 10,000 employees across Canada, has also prohibited smoking in all work areas. This is an essential first step for a department that should properly be in the forefront of the move towards healthier workplaces. But here again, unfortunately, an otherwise admirable policy is marred by permitting smoking in designated areas and allowing the contaminants to find their way into the central air supply. It's to be hoped that Health and Welfare Canada, and all other employers who care enough to ban smoking in work areas, will eventually decide to take that necessary additional step. If smoking is to be permitted in designated areas, those areas should be separately ventilated.

Giant Boeing Company has announced that it is moving toward a total ban on smoking for all its 95,000 employees in the United States. A new interim policy restricts smoking in common areas and allows employees to designate their work stations as No Smoking areas. Said a Boeing spokesman: "We haven't done any studies, but we do know we lose work time through smoking and we're trying to hold down medical costs due to smoking-related illness. The company is very determined to move ahead on this. We've considered various policies and decided that the best of all possible worlds would be a total ban." [86]

The List Grows

The movement is gathering speed across Canada as company after company implements measures to clear the air. A common policy is to ban smoking in work areas and restrict it to designated locations such as lounges or sections of the cafeteria. While this is not a recommended approach, since smoke generated in such places usually finds its way into the central air supply, it is an improvement over uncontrolled smoking. Breaking the habit of smoking in work areas makes it easier to move eventually to a better solution – separately ventilated smoking areas, or best, a complete ban on the premises.

The insurance industry, in particular, is showing leadership in this direction, probably because it understands the human costs better than others. Among the companies that have banned smoking in the workplace or plan to do so are the Insurance Corporation of British Columbia (2,300 employees); Aetna Canada of Toronto (1,250 employees); Halifax Insurance Companies of Toronto; Safeco Insurance Companies of Streetsville, Ont.; and North American Life Assurance Co. of Toronto.

The smoke-filled newsroom is also going the way of the old hot-lead linotype. The *Whig-Standard* in Kingston, Ont. has banned smoking from its workplace, as have the *Recorder* and *Times* in Brockville, Ont., and the tiny *Economist* and *Sun* in Markham, Ontario. The Toronto *Globe and Mail* has announced plans for a total workplace ban, and no one is allowed to smoke in the newsroom at CBC national radio in Toronto.

Other Canadian organizations that have cleared the air are Maritime Telephone and Telegraph Co. Ltd. of Halifax (3,600 employees); Town and Country shops (1,200 employees across Canada); Bata Shoes (Toronto world headquarters building); Concord Scientific Corp. of Toronto; Misericordia Hospital in Edmonton; General Hospital in Ottawa.

This, of course, is nothing like a comprehensive list; these are simply among the organizations whose smoking policies have come to our attention.

Smokers Vote 'Yes'

> *"'No Smoking' signs are becoming increasingly popular in Canada's workplaces, as evidence piles up showing smoking on the job may be more than just a nuisance. And companies banning smoking report few staff problems because of the policy." – Worklife magazine.*

A worry among some employers contemplating a smoking policy for the first time is that restrictions might destroy morale by setting smokers and nonsmokers against each other, or that smoking employees might become disgruntled and unco-operative. But experience has shown almost the opposite to be the case. Whenever a work force has been surveyed following implementation of a smoking policy, employees have registered a high level of satisfaction with it – and this includes smoking employees.

When the British Columbia Ministry of Health introduced the smoking policy described above, the regulations were voluntary. Compliance was good to begin with, but smokers gradually began to ignore the rules. After six months of declining compliance, management asked the work force if it should introduce a compulsory policy. Seventy per cent, including smokers, said "yes." According to a spokesman, compliance has been excellent ever since, and there are no problems. [87]

Three weeks after Health and Welfare Canada banned smoking for its 10,000 employees, a spokesman was able to report: "The policy is working very, very well. No one's panicked yet."

The Auditor-General's department, with its tough no-smoking rule, reports full compliance. Said a spokesman: "Everyone is just delighted, even the smokers. Some have said to me, 'That's just the kick in the pants I needed. It's helped me to cut down.'"

It's been the same for the Department of Regional Industrial Expansion, where a spokesman said, "There hasn't been a single grievance. That speaks for itself." Two weeks after the ban was instituted, the department carried out a productivity survey. It showed that, on average, 27 people were using the smoking areas at any one time – which is less than 2 per cent of the work force.

"A majority of them were taking work with them so they weren't wasting time," according to the spokesman. "That was just after the ban was imposed; there wouldn't be as many smokers out there now. And we're seeing the benefits. Tests have shown that particulates in the air are down 70 per cent since we banned smoking."

Canada's private employers are also discovering that smoking bans make for a happier workplace. "I've not spoken to anyone who finds it a problem," said a personnel officer with Safeco Insurance. "People took it well. There've been no problems," said a spokesman for the Halifax Insurance Companies. After introducing a smoking policy for 7,000 employees in its Consumer Products Division, Pratt and Whitney Aircraft Co. found such a high level of satisfaction among employees – smokers as well as nonsmokers – that it was planning to extend the policy to 40,000 employees in three divisions. [88]

Robert Rosner, a Seattle consultant on workplace smoking policies, reports the experience of a Washington state health co-operative that instituted a total ban for 6,000 employees in 23 locations: "It was very controversial at first. Upper management was scared; they were afraid it would be very disruptive. Six months after the policy was implemented the controversy was gone. The company has since taken a survey and found that 85 per cent of its employees support the policy. In a year I'm sure it will be pushing 95 per cent." [89]

> *"Smokers, no doubt cowed by official warnings that they could be puffing disease down the throats of their neighbors, by and large meekly submit to no-smoking-on-the-job rules. They ask only to be left to puff in peace off the job."* – Wall Street Journal. [90]

The Kansas Department of Health and Environment banned smoking for its 600 employees after a survey showed that the move was favored by a majority of smokers as well as nonsmokers. Management reports that the policy is running smoothly, with only "isolated" problems, and that smokers themselves are generally satisfied with the ban. [91]

And then there are the foot-draggers. An employee of Citadel Life Assurance Co. in Toronto, asked whether there was a smoking policy in her workplace, could only reply: "I wish there were!"

Far from destroying morale, it turns out that strong smoking policies actually improve it. Nonsmokers are happier, for a start, and smokers themselves tend to welcome a measure which makes the workplace healthier for themselves. And both are grateful for the lessening of tensions that comes with well-defined rules. A smoking policy clears the air in the workplace in more ways than one!

And It Pays

In an article under the heading "No Smoking – Business Finds It Profitable," the respected *Christian Science Monitor* reports: "It costs the George W. Dahl Co. of Bristol, Rhode Island, more than $8,000 a year to pay its nonsmokers $3 a week to refrain. But the increased productivity from healthy and busy workers justifies the expense, says a company spokesman." [92]

Even small companies profit when the No Smoking signs go up. After a smoker started a potentially dangerous fire in a wastepaper basket, Qualitype Co. of Toronto instituted a total ban for its 23 employees.

"We used to find cigarette butts on the side of a press, or by the computer," remembers company president Gordon Krull. "That kind of carelessness could have cost all of us our jobs. Now I've worked it out that we save $800 a year on insurance. We save another $10 a week on cleaning costs. Cleaner air means reduced computer maintenance costs, which I calculate at $1,500 a year. And there have been great savings from reduced absenteeism."

He says employees are allowed to go outside to smoke, but it has become "socially unacceptable" to leave others to do the work. The result is that all but two smokers have quit, and those who continue to smoke say the ban helps them reduce their consumption. [93]

Here, illustrating a different kind of saving, is part of a letter. It was written by Aetna janitorial service in Washington state to a large client, Unigard Insurance Group, which had instituted a smoking ban in its offices. "Prior to [the ban]," said the letter, "each smoker's desk had an ashtray to clean as well as ashes spread over the desktops and on the carpet around the desk...We now don't have to dump and clean the ashtrays. The dusting of desktops is easier. Carpets don't need to be edged or shampooed as often. Upholstered furniture is easier to keep clean. Windows don't get dirty as fast, and frequencies [of cleaning] have been reduced." Because cleaning took less time, the letter explained, the janitorial service had been able to reduce its charges for the month of April, 1982, by $866. And the rebate cheque attached to the letter was unsolicited! [94]

6

THE GREAT 'RIGHTS' DEBATE

It's been shown that there is only one way to protect the health of nonsmokers in the workplace. It is to ban smoking altogether – or, as a second-best solution, to restrict it to separately ventilated smoking lounges. But any attempt to curtail smoking inevitably runs into the cry: What about the rights of smokers? What about freedom of choice?

The chief champion of the so-called right to smoke is, as you might expect, the tobacco industry. Here's how the matter was expressed several years ago by Paul Paré, then president of Imperial Tobacco Ltd. and now chairman of its parent, Imasco Ltd. He was reacting to proposals by a Parliamentary committee to curb tobacco advertising in Canada.

"The committee fails to recognize," said Mr. Paré, "that there are two large groups of Canadians, each with their rights and privileges. One group is composed of nonsmokers. The others are those Canadians who choose to use tobacco and cigarettes as a part of their pattern of living for relaxation, stimulation and enjoyment. The committee's proposals would set about to eliminate their freedom of choice in this matter of tobacco use... Who knows what custom or personal activity may be next?" [95]

And here, from a recent magazine advertisement, is a "message to nonsmokers" from the United States Tobacco Institute:

Smoking is "a small ritual that welcomes strangers, provides companion-ship in solitude, fills empty time, marks the significance of certain occasions and expresses personal style. For **some** people. And by personal choice, not for you. That's the way it ought to be. Whether your preference is carrot juice or bottled water, beach buggies or foreign cars, tobacco smoking or chewing gum or none of the above. Personal style." [96]

Behind the chatty tone lie several messages. The industry wants the public to believe that:

• There is a right to smoke.

• Smoking is a personal matter.

• It's a matter of freedom of choice.

• It is a friendly, harmless pastime.

By hammering away at such themes in its advertising and publicity efforts, the tobacco industry has managed to persuade a lot of people that the debate over second-hand smoke is not about health at all, but about individual rights and freedoms. The notion is clearly nonsensical, but nonsmokers have to be able to show it to be so. Let's look at the tobacco industry's messages one by one.

'There is a Right to Smoke'

> "A patient with tuberculosis has the right to cough, but not in anyone else's face."
> — Dr. Peter Morgan, Scientific Editor,
> Canadian Medical Association Journal. [97]

When the tobacco industry or smokers themselves say there is a right to smoke, they are talking in code. They are not really asserting a right to smoke, for it's generally conceded that people have every right to do so – just as they have every right to drink pop, chew gum or beat themselves over the head with a board. What they are asserting is a right to smoke **at will** – that is, to smoke without regard for the consequences to others. They are claiming a right to pollute – and the long and the short of it is that there is no such right in society.

"I assert," writes Repace, "that smokers have the right to enjoy the risks and benefits [?] of smoking, just as they have the right to play Russian roulette. When they smoke indoors in the presence of others, however, they are playing Russian roulette with nonsmokers' health. This they do not have the right to do." [98]

Put another way, we have every right to walk down the street, but not to walk on our neighbor's flower bed. We can use a power mower all day long, but not at night when that same neighbor is trying to sleep. We can get drunk, but we can't endanger someone else's life by getting behind the wheel of a car.

"It would be misdirected to equate the 'right' to smoke with such fundamental civil liberties as the right of free speech, the right of assembly, freedom of religion, etc.," writes Walter Tarnopolsky, a professor of law and former president of the Canadian Civil Liberties Association. "A person's freedom to act must certainly be limited when such acts injure or tend to injure others. The claim of a person to a right to unpolluted air must take precedence over a claim to a right to smoke in public....

"A person's 'right' to smoke might more accurately be described as a limited privilege..." [emphasis added] (It's worth mentioning that Professor Tarnopolsky is himself a smoker – or at least he was when this statement was written.) [99]

'Smoking is a Personal Matter'

"Personal style," says the Tobacco Institute ad. "Whether your preference is carrot juice or bottled water, beach buggies or foreign cars, tobacco smoking or chewing gum or none of the above."

Clearly, most of these choices are personal; whether one chooses carrot juice or bottled water bothers no one else and therefore concerns no one else. But how personal can smoking be when it is routinely carried out in the presence of others? When, as we saw in an earlier section, only a small fraction of the smoke produced by a cigarette is consumed directly by the smoker and the rest is discharged into the common air for others to breathe? When the health consequences are routinely visited on others?

If smokers want smoking to be regarded as a personal matter, they should make it so. In the meantime, sad to say, it remains very much a public matter.

'It's a Matter of Freedom of Choice'

> *"People must be free to choose... PROVIDED IT IS AN INFORMED CHOICE. That choice is hopelessly prejudiced if it has to be made against the constant pressure of sales promotion, always presenting smoking as a sociable, attractive activity of normal men and women in pleasant circumstances. By now we have come to realize that smoking is essentially a form of addiction, which is cleverly reinforced by sales promotion."*
>
> – Dr. George Godber,
> former Chief Medical Officer of England. [100]

The great and glaring irony of the tobacco industry's constant reference to freedom of choice is that, where its products are concerned, accustomed users have woefully little choice in the matter. Nicotine is one of the most fiercely addictive substances on earth. According to the American Psychiatric Association, in its Diagnostic and Statistical Manual of Mental Disorders, regular smokers suffer from "a dependence disorder" – a designation which places smoking in a family of dependence disorders that includes alcoholism and heroin addiction. "In fact, as measured by inability to abstain," observes William Pollin, director of the U.S. National Institute on Drug Abuse, "**smoking is much more addictive than alcohol** [emphasis added]." [101] Researchers have also found that is it more resistant to treatment than heroin addiction. [102]

It might be argued that people are at least free to decide whether to **start** smoking. But even that isn't so. Most people who become smokers do so well before the age of independent choice, at a time in their lives when they are most vulnerable to peer pressure and the seductive images of the tobacco ads.

Health and Welfare Canada reports that nine per cent of boys and 13 per cent of girls are already **daily** smokers by the time they are 12 to 14 years old. The percentage is up to 29 per cent for both sexes in the 15 to 17 age bracket. By ages 18 to 19, fully 38 per cent of boys and 40 per cent of girls are daily smokers. By the late teens smoking rates have already reached the rate for the general population. [103]

What this shows, all too clearly, is that the tobacco industry has fully captured its clientele before they have reached adulthood – before, in fact, they are allowed by law to take their first drink! The information that the smoking rates for 19-year-olds are somewhat higher than the general rate makes the additional point that the clientele drops off as it gets older. When people do have mature freedom of choice, in other words, they are more likely to choose **not** to smoke!

'Smoking is a Friendly, Harmless Pastime'

"A small ritual," says the tobacco ad, "that welcomes strangers, provides companionship in solitude, fills empty time, marks the significance of certain occasions..."

The ad certainly makes smoking seem harmless enough. And it's true that smokers don't begin to reel wildly about after a few puffs; they don't have to embark on a life of crime to support the practice; they still go to work and still function as ordinary members of society. Yet, while all of this is true, epidemiologists will confirm a single and inescapable fact: **Smoking is the most widespread and destructive drug addiction ever seen on the face of the earth.**

Consider, to begin with, the numbers immediately involved. Here, according to the best estimates, is how many Canadians suffer from our three major dependence disorders:

Illicit drugs	13,000 [104]
Alcohol	600,000 [105]
Nicotine	7,300,000 [106]

While tobacco works more slowly than alcohol and hard drugs, it works surely – and in the end reaps the greater harvest. "Tobacco is known to be associated with more deaths and illnesses than any other single product," begins a 1983 report prepared for Health and Welfare Canada's Bureau of Tobacco Control and Biometrics under the title "Dollar Estimates of the Consequences of Tobacco Use in Canada, 1979." [107]

Here, side by side, are recent annual mortality estimates for Canada's three big addictions:

Deaths related to illicit drugs	544 [108]
Deaths related to alcoholism and alcohol-related road accidents	17,974 [see footnote]
Deaths attributable to smoking	28,700 [109]

Source: "Alcoholism in Canada: A National Perspective," Health and Welfare Canada, 1984, p. 33. Total alcohol-related deaths referred to above cover the year 1980 and include deaths from road accidents, falls, fires, drownings, homicides and suicides (total: 5,554) as well as from certain categories of circulatory and respiratory disease and cancer (10,310). Deaths from conditions considered **directly** attributable to alcohol use – cirrhosis, alcohol dependency syndrome, non-dependent abuse of alcohol, alcoholic psychosis and accidental alcohol poisoning – numbered 2,110 in 1980.

TOBACCO'S 'CONTRIBUTION'

Then there are the economic costs of smoking. Here, according to the Health and Welfare Canada report cited above, was the drain on the economy for one year (1979):

Consequences:	Costs: (millions of dollars)
• Lost income due to early deaths	$3,361
• 45.5 million lost working days	616
• 1,925,000 days of hospitalization	1,096
• Doctor visits	22
• Fires	85
Total costs in 1979 dollars	$5.2 billion

It should be noted that these statistics on mortality and economic loss don't begin to count the true cost to Canadian society. They don't include illness, disability, lowered productivity and absenteeism among nonsmokers whose health is impaired by regular exposure to tobacco smoke – and they don't begin to reckon the human suffering that underlies the statistics. A "small ritual" indeed!

Before leaving the subject of economic costs, let us take a moment to deal with the tobacco industry's oft-repeated assertion that smoking makes a positive contribution to Canada by creating jobs and providing a large tax source. This contribution, according to the Health and Welfare report, came to $3 billion in 1979 – over half of it in the form of taxes. As we've just seen, however, smoking-related **costs** amounted to $5.2 billion in that same year. The balance sheet thus shows a net loss to Canadian society of $2.2 billion.

The industry continues nonetheless to make a great deal of the billions of dollars spent on tobacco products, and indeed uses such figures as a form of blackmail. A frequently heard assertion is that, if governments continue to put obstacles in the way of selling cigarettes – or if, heaven forbid, the industry should be forced out of business – Canada would lose all those jobs and all that beautiful tax money. But it just isn't so. Here is how the matter was explained in a House of Commons report which called on Ottawa to place severe limitations on tobacco advertising: "Since cigarettes are a consumer good and not a basic resource, the domestic tobacco economy is supported by out-of-pocket purchases by smokers. This money would not disappear from the economy but would be available for the purchases of other goods, subject to some or all of the same taxes as cigarettes." [110]

In short, the money that now supports jobs in the tobacco industry would be used to create jobs in other industries. Not only would Canada reap the benefits of that new economic activity, it would also be spared the health costs and other economic losses now associated with smoking. The net gain would be incalculable.

7

TOBACCO AND THE LAW

One of the earliest attempts to control the use of tobacco by legislative means was the imposition of special import duties by King James I of England in the early 1600s. The King, who might be considered history's first nonsmokers' rights activist, sought to check the spread of a custom that had recently been introduced from the New World by way of Spain and France and was already turning the air blue in London's coffee houses and fashionable parlors.

But it was already too late. One of the most addictive substances ever seen on earth had already established its grip on the country. As Francis Bacon observed: "In our times the use of tobacco is growing greatly and conquers men with a certain sweet pleasure, so that those who have once become accustomed thereto can later hardly be restrained therefrom." As smoking continued to make inroads on the Continent, its addictive characteristic was further noted by a Dutch writer who described it as "a sort of smoke-tippling, one might call it, which enslaves its victims more completely than any other form of intoxication, old or new." [111]

"Between the 16th and 17th centuries it conquered the whole world," writes French historian Fernand Braudel. "We get our information about the early use of tobacco from violent government prohibitions (governments later came to realize the attractive possibilities of financial return and the Tobacco Monopoly was established in France in 1674). These prohibitions encircled the world: England 1604, Japan 1607-9, the Ottoman Empire 1611, the Mogul Empire 1617, Sweden and Denmark 1632, Russia 1634, Naples 1637, Sicily 1640, China 1642, the Papal States 1642, the Electorate of Cologne 1649, Wurttemberg 1651." [112]

Prohibitions were backed by a wide range of penalties, many of them excessive by the standards of any day. Some are listed by Tobacco King Alfred Dunhill in a book bearing the somewhat self-serving title, *The Gentle Art of Smoking:* "In Turkey, because smoking was not sanctioned by the Koran, it was thought fit only for the Christian dog, and some offenders, with pipes thrust through their noses, were led on mules through the streets. A Chinese decree of 1638 threatened decapitation to anyone who trafficked in tobacco. Russian offenders were deported to Siberia, and some

Tsars submitted them to torture and even to death. In parts of Europe the penalties were less lethal, but many bans were passed, especially by various Popes who threatened offenders with excommunication." [113] But edicts and punishments alike were ignored, notes Braudel, particularly in China: "By the end of the 18th Century everyone in China smoked – men and women, mandarins and poor, down to toddlers two feet high." [114]

THE AGE OF THE CIGARETTE

Throughout most of its long and sorry history, tobacco was consumed mostly in pipes and cigars or in the form of chewing tobacco and snuff. Then in the late 1800s came a portentous development – automatic cigarette-making machines. The cost of smoking dropped dramatically. And because cigarette tobacco was less harsh than earlier forms, nicotine could now be "mainlined" by drawing smoke deeply into the lungs. This made smoking much more satisfying – and powerfully more addictive. Less-harsh fumes made smoking more socially acceptable at the same time, and women began to take up what seemed to them a chic new practice. In the United States alone, cigarette production soared between 1880 and 1895 from 500 million to 4 billion. [115]

The consumption curve continued its dizzy climb as succeeding generations became ever more heavily hooked. By 1982 Americans were smoking 635 **billion** cigarettes a year! In Britain, the figure for 1981 was 110 billion. [116] And the historic pattern can also be seen clearly in this country. In 1920 Canadians smoked 3 billion cigarettes, or about one a day per adult. By 1973 it was close to 55 billion, or about nine a day per adult [117] , and a decade later consumption had reached more than 63 billion cigarettes. [118]

What were governments doing while cigarettes ensnared whole generations? Virtually nothing. There was a spate of anti-smoking legislation in North America around the turn of the century, but it was enacted for the wrong reasons. Authorities, backed by some church leaders and abolitionist groups, sought to curb tobacco use on the grounds that it was sinful, besides being a fire hazard. No thought was given to the health of smokers, still less to that of exposed nonsmokers. Gradually, these misconceived statutes dropped from sight. By the 1950s, anti-smoking laws had become a rarity. The cigarette was king, and smoke was everywhere.

THE TIDE TURNS

"America, once described by Charles Dickens as 'one vast expectoration,' gradually eliminated public spitting. Arguments against controls were much like those used against smoking limits today. When the Pennsylvania legislature in 1904 passed legislation controlling spitting, Gov. Samuel Pennypacker vetoed it, declaring: 'It is a gentleman's constitutional right to expectorate.' But the spittoon has disappeared from the business office and the factory floor."
– Regina Carlson. [119]

The 1960s saw an historic turning point. At the beginning of the decade, smoking was still socially acceptable. Then, quite suddenly, alarm bells started ringing as medical authorities around the world began to point to accumulating evidence that more and more conclusively identified cigarettes as a leading cause of early death among smokers. Later came the first indications that nonsmokers were also at risk from second-hand smoke.

Today tobacco stands indicted as a serious health hazard to all who are exposed to it, and its social acceptability is sharply on the wane in most industrialized countries. Although the world will continue to pay the health costs for decades to come, it seems safe to say that in the 1980s – nearly four centuries after tobacco use first spread from the New World to the Old – we are witnessing the beginning of the end of an epidemic that has inflicted untold suffering on humankind.

The change in the public perception of smoking has been reflected in a reborn willingness of governments in North America to legislate in the area of smoking and health, but the new laws are significantly different from those passed in the early part of the century. Comments Morley Swingle in the *Missouri Law Review:* "When the early laws were enacted, cigarette smoke had not been proven dangerous to humans. Today that danger is widely recognized. While the early statutes were enacted largely to enforce moral behavior and to prevent fire hazards, the recent statutes are specifically designed to protect people from the health dangers of cigarette smoke.

"Also, while the older statutes were aimed at prohibiting all cigarette smoking, modern statutes seek only to protect people in public places from the smoke of others. **The modern statutes, unlike the over-broad early laws, are probably here to stay** [emphasis added]." [120]

The drive to protect indoor air quality through statute and governmental regulation is accelerating, particularly in the United States. By the beginning of the 1980s, 34 states had passed legislation giving at least some protection to nonsmokers. [121] According to Swingle: "Twenty-four states and the District of Columbia prohibit smoking in public transportation; 24 prohibit smoking in elevators; 23 prohibit smoking in public waiting rooms or various other parts of health care facilities; 21 prohibit smoking in places of recreation or entertainment, like libraries, museums, theatres, lecture or concert halls, auditoriums, or swimming pools; 15 prohibit smoking in public schools; 12 prohibit smoking in state-owned buildings; 11 prohibit smoking in public meetings; nine restrict smoking in restaurants; seven prohibit smoking in supermarkets or food stores; six prohibit smoking in public department stores; six prohibit smoking in any place where the proprietor has posted a No Smoking sign; and six prohibit smoking in *any* public place 'including but not limited to' a list of specified places." [122]

MOVING INTO THE WORKPLACE

Four states have taken the matter a valuable and necessary step further, enacting comprehensive legislation which extends smoking controls to the workplace. A leader in this area is Minnesota. Under the state's *Clean Indoor Air Act (1975),* "the department of labor and industry shall, in consultation with the state board of health, establish rules to restrict or prohibit smoking in those places of work where the close proximation of workers or the inadequacy of ventilation causes smoke pollution detrimental to the health and comfort of nonsmoking employees." The effect is to ban smoking in all enclosed working spaces except areas specially designated for smokers.

Local Strides

At the local level, some far-reaching workplace legislation has been passed in California. San Francisco led the way in 1983 in the face of massive opposition from the tobacco industry. The city's ordinance, designed "to minimize the toxic effects of smoking in the office workplace," requires "(1) that the employer make accommodations for the preferences of both nonsmoking and smoking employees, and (2) **if a satisfactory accommodation to all affected employees cannot be reached, that the employer prohibit smoking in the office workplace** [emphasis added]." [123]

The city of Pasadena followed suit in the spring of 1984 with a unanimous decision to add a new chapter to its Municipal Code. According to the preamble, "The [Pasadena] Board of Directors finds that the smoking of tobacco, or any other weed or plant, is a positive danger to health and a material annoyance, inconvenience, discomfort and a health hazard to those who are present in confined spaces, and in order to serve public health, safety and welfare, the declared purpose of this Chapter 8.78 is to prohibit the smoking of tobacco, or any weed or plant, in public places and places of employment..."

After prohibiting or regulating smoking in a wide variety of public places, the ordinance requires every employer to adopt a written policy on workplace smoking to contain, at a minimum, the following:

1. Prohibition of smoking in employer conference and meeting rooms, classrooms, auditoriums, restrooms, medical facilities, hallways and elevators.

2. Provision and maintenance of contiguous No Smoking area of not less than one-half of the seating capacity and floor space in cafeterias, lunchrooms and employee lounges.

3. Any employee in the office workplace shall be given the right to designate his or her immediate work area as a nonsmoking area and to post it with appropriate signs or sign. The policy adopted by the employer shall include a definition of the term "immediate work area" which gives preferential consideration to nonsmokers.

The crucial provision is found in Para. B (Sec. 8.78.100): **"In any dispute arising under the smoking policy, the rights of the nonsmoker shall be given precedence** [emphasis added]." [124]

Los Angeles adopted a smoking ordinance of its own in late 1984. The intention of its sponsors was to imitate the San Francisco and Pasadena ordinances by making the interests of nonsmokers paramount, but the regulation was watered down after a political fight that saw an important behind-the-scenes intervention by the tobacco industry. As it turned out, Los Angeles requires merely that employers make "reasonable" efforts to create nonsmoking areas. [125]

AND IN CANADA

If we have been dwelling overlong on U.S. examples, the reason once again is that the United States has been setting the pace. Where the Americans have been pushing ahead, Canadian legislators have been cautiously feeling their way. As yet there is nothing in this country resembling state-wide legislation on smoking. Instead we have a proliferation of municipal bylaws of greater or lesser effectiveness.

One of the better Canadian examples is provided by Hamilton, Ontario. Like many other Canadian cities, it prohibits smoking in such places as doctors' waiting rooms, customer service areas, line-ups, elevators, theatres and stores. But Hamilton goes further than most other communities by requiring that restaurants set aside a minimum percentage of seats for nonsmokers and, of critical importance, it provides that those who own and manage premises covered in the bylaw share some responsibility for its enforcement.

NO REVOLUTIONS

The most noteworthy and heartening feature of all these latter-day government interventions is that they have invariably met with broad public acceptance – and have generally been accepted with equanimity and even approval by smokers themselves.

In the Toronto survey of public attitudes towards smoking, referred to earlier, 484 smokers were asked how they would react to **more** nonsmoking areas in public places. While 14 per cent said they would consider it an intrusion on their liberty, nearly half said they wouldn't care either way. More interestingly still, fully 37 per cent of smokers said they would welcome more regulations – it would help them to quit! [126]

Similarly, a survey commissioned by the Minneapolis *Tribune* found that 92 per cent of the population was in favor of the Minnesota *Clean Indoor Air Act*, with its restrictions on workplace smoking, and this included 87 per cent of those describing themselves as heavy smokers! [127]

San Francisco's experience has been enlightening. Although the tobacco industry predicted that a massive and costly bureaucracy would be required to enforce the workplace ordinance and arbitrate disputes between smokers and nonsmokers, the "bureaucracy" consists of one inspector working half-time on enforcement. No more are needed because the city has found that, with legislation in place, smoking and nonsmoking employees are almost always able to reach agreement without reference to outside authority.

Comments Frank Patane, San Francisco's principal environmental health inspector: "It's running the way most of our laws do, with a minimum of effort and a maximum of compliance. We're very pleased." [128]

Pasadena has had the same experience with its own workplace ordinance. Noted an official in the city's Health Department: "I'd be surprised if we've had two complaints in the last eight months." [129]

Far from being disruptive, as it turns out, legislated smoking restrictions actually improve relations between smokers and nonsmokers by establishing ground rules and defining respective rights and responsibilities. But to give smokers full credit, the main reason that they have tended to accept legislated restrictions, once in place, is almost certainly their acknowledgment, however reluctant, that these restrictions are essentially fair-minded. **Let the tobacco industry rant and rave about "freedom to smoke" as it seeks to shore up sagging markets; smokers themselves are aware that the demand of fellow citizens for breathable air is logically unchallengeable.**

Much has changed, thank goodness, since the days when smokers were led through the streets on mules and crusaders denounced smoking as a sin. Instead of anti-**smoking** laws, governments are starting to pass anti-**smoke** laws. Instead of a prohibitionist movement, we have what might be called a freedom movement – one that fully recognizes the right of individuals to smoke as long as they don't deprive others of the right not to.

8

TOBACCO AND THE COURTS

> "[Traditionally recognized workplace hazards] may well be the cause of long-term damaging effects on health. Even so, none of these problems have the potential that cigarette smoking has for causing employee discord... It may well be that measures can be taken to satisfy smokers as well as nonsmokers... But if this is not possible, both the union and the employer are in an unenviable position: One group or the other is likely to sue, and to resent whatever action the union or employer take.
>
> "As a legal matter, however, taking into account current medical opinion, it looks as though the nonsmokers will prevail in the event of a clear-cut conflict [emphasis added]." – Labor Law News [130]

Timothy J. Lowenberg, a U.S. labor lawyer, notes that "most courts have ruled since well before the turn of the century that an employer has a continuing, affirmative duty to provide a safe and healthful place of work." [131]

This duty has traditionally been interpreted by judges as meaning that a workplace must be reasonably free from physical hazards – unguarded saws, exposed wiring etc. – and things like harmful industrial chemicals. The idea that tobacco smoke is a hazardous workplace substance was rarely considered. Then came the celebrated case of SHIMP vs. NEW JERSEY BELL in 1976.

A 15-year Bell employee with a good record, Donna Shimp suffered severe allergic reactions even to low concentrations of tobacco smoke. She put up with it until she was transferred to a poorly ventilated office where seven out of 13 employees were heavy smokers. After a series of formal complaints to management, she was offered a job switch that involved a demotion and lower pay. Mrs. Shimp refused to accept what she considered to be a penalty. After exhausting all remaining grievance procedures, she launched suit in New Jersey Superior Court.

The judgment ordered Bell to provide Mrs. Shimp with safe working conditions, specifically by prohibiting smoking in its offices and customer service area. What made the ruling so significant is that it was based, not primarily on Mrs. Shimp's allergy, but on common law principles applicable to non-smokers in general. Since the judgment has become a legal landmark in

North America, it is worth quoting at some length:

"It is clearly the law in this state that an employee has a right to work in a safe environment. An employer is under an affirmative duty to provide a work area that is free from unsafe conditions...The evidence is clear and overwhelming. Cigarette smoke contaminates and pollutes the air, creating a health hazard not merely to the smoker but to all those around [him or her] who must rely upon the same air supply.

"The right of an individual to risk his or her health does not include the right to jeopardize the health of those who must remain around him or her in order to properly perform the duties of their jobs."

It was noted with some irony that New Jersey Bell didn't permit smoking near switching equipment – a rule which probably was fatal to the company's case. "The rationale behind the rule," said the judgment, "is that the machines are extremely sensitive and can be damaged by the smoke. Human beings are also very sensitive and can be damaged by cigarette smoke." [132]

"Although SHIMP is a New Jersey case," writes Morley Swingle, "it offers strong precedent for nonsmoking workers in other jurisdictions...Of particular precedential value in SHIMP are the strong statements of legal recognition of the dangers of cigarette smoke...The strong language of SHIMP and the ever-increasing medical evidence of the danger of involuntary smoking may be enough to persuade [another] court of the real danger involved...The New Jersey court recognized the danger of tobacco smoke to nonsmokers in general, as well as to those with allergies." [133]

The common law principle was restated by the Missouri Court of Appeal in a suit brought by nonsmoker Paul Smith against Western Electric. "It is well-settled in Missouri," said the judgment, "that an employer owes a duty to the employee to use all reasonable care to provide a reasonably safe workplace...and to protect the employee from avoidable perils." [134]

In a brief presented during the Missouri trial, law professor Alvan Brody argued that common law principles don't require that a nonsmoker prove health damage from second-hand smoke. "One of the most basic of these principles is the inviolability of one's body," he writes. "Intrusions far more limited in scope have evoked judicial response in a wide variety of contexts. Even if the hazards of second-hand smoke were trivial, the court should still protect against them. It should make no difference whether third parties give a plaintiff black eyes or red ones." How much more compelling is the argument when, as Prof. Brody goes on to observe, the hazards are anything but trivial. [135]

BETTER LATE THAN NEVER

"During the last decade, nonsmokers have tested the water in a new area of law, with the clear result that remedies now exist for the nonsmoker who cares enough about his rights to seek legal help."
– Morley Swingle [136]

We have been citing U.S. court cases because experience in that country is running ahead of our own. But the precedents being established there will inevitably have a bearing on how Canadian courts react to workplace suits, more particularly where U.S. cases have been fought on the principles of common law (the body of law based on past court decisions), as opposed to statutory law (laws passed by legislative bodies). Canada and the United States share the common law tradition, and court decisions based on common law have precedential value on either side of the border. The *Labor Law News* underlines this point when it says:

"It can be expected that employees in Canada, as in the U.S., will go to court to stop smoking at the workplace on the basis of their common law right to a safe working environment. There is no doubt that there is such a right here in Canada as in the United States. As the Ontario Court of Appeal recently stated in BERGER vs. WILLOWDALE A.M.C.: "...an employer owes a duty to its employee of providing and maintaining a safe working place..." [137]

"What position will the courts take on tobacco smoking?" the review asks. "One indication may be the following comment of the Ontario Supreme Court in a 1979 case in which the court rejected a challenge to municipal bylaws prohibiting smoking in public places:

"'...the common law right of the smoker to smoke and the common law right of the proprietor to carry on business without restrictions must be subject to the right of their neighbors to good health, free from the health hazard or discomfort occasioned by second-hand smoke.'" [138]

Here again, this time in the words of the Ontario Supreme Court, there emerges the important idea that common law rights are not limited to protection from **health hazards** associated with second-hand smoke. Individuals also have the right to be spared unnecessary **discomfort** in carrying out their work.

A CONTINENT-WIDE MOVEMENT

Quite clearly, North American courts are moving towards an interpretation of the common law which recognizes tobacco smoke as an **unnecessary** workplace hazard – as distinct from a hazard that is essential to a production process – and which recognizes the duty of employers to protect nonsmokers from this hazard.

"Make no mistake about it," advises labor lawyer Lowenberg. "Many employers have attempted to remain on the sidelines and assume the posture of a disinterested observer in the so-called fight between smoking and nonsmoking employees. Many employers have justified their inaction by claiming that they are under an affirmative obligation to protect the rights of smokers as much as nonsmokers – and that, in considering a smoking policy for their company they must, as a matter of law, try to strike a balance between the rights of smokers and the rights of nonsmokers. This fence-straddling policy is a fallacious one because it rests upon a fundamentally unsound premise; that is, that smokers have a legal right to smoke in the workplace...

47

"The handwriting is on the wall, and employers are no longer going to be able to remain on the sidelines because, in fact, their inaction is as decisive as intentionally striking a balance in favor of the smoker. Employers who have not ensured a smoke-free environment for their nonsmoking employees are increasingly paying higher premiums because of work-men's compensation, disability and unemployment compensation awards, as well as other penalties in civil suits. There are no comparable economic penalties when the employer protects the acknowledged rights of nonsmoking employees. [*See footnote*]

"There is nothing in our common law system," Lowenberg continues, "which indicates that there is any more of a right to smoke in the workplace than there is a right to sing at the top of one's voice or to dress however one wishes or to play one's personal radio in whatever manner one wishes or to do anything else which is not necessary to the performance of the essential elements of an assigned job." [139]

WAFFLING ON COMPENSATION

The passive smoking issue is one that has caused excruciating problems for workers' compensation authorities. They are confronted by a mountain of scientific evidence establishing beyond a shade of doubt that tobacco smoke is a dangerous substance, one that can and does cause disease and lung impairment in nonsmokers. Yet, fearful of setting a precedent which might open a floodgate of claims, they have consistently refused to recognize tobacco smoke as an occupational hazard – even at the cost of denying the evidence in front of them.

Dust, Not Smoke

Murdeena Johnson is a nonsmoker who quit her job with a Toronto utility company after developing asthma. She claimed workers' compensation on the grounds that the disease had been caused by "tobacco smoke and dust" in her workplace. Her doctor, she wrote, "would not consent to my return to work unless smoking was restricted." Elsewhere she testified that "the office environment, heavily laden with smoke, was constantly distressing."

Compensation was eventually granted, but not without some cautious wriggling on the part of the claims ajudicator. "It is considered that Mrs. Johnson's reactivity to tobacco smoke is not an occupationally derived phenomena [sic], but it has been one factor in several together, accounting for her manifest asthma," he wrote. "It was recommended that we accept responsibility in this claim, NOT BECAUSE OF TOBACCO SMOKE PER-SE [emphasis added], but because there was

Footnote: Some of Lowenberg's observations do not apply directly to the Canadian situation, where employees generally have no right to sue their employers for injuries covered by workers' compensation. But when nonsmoking employees start making claims against compensation plans, Canadian employers will certainly have to foot a healthy share of the bill.

enough evidence in the consultant's view of unusually high concentration of dust and tobacco smoke . . ."

Tobacco smoke, which had received pride of place in Mrs. Johnson's application for compensation, had now officially become a secondary source of blame. When the press drew its own conclusions nonetheless, hailing the decision as a precedent for nonsmoking employees, a Compensation Board official rushed forward with a further disclaimer which, in effect, disowned the ajudicator's ruling: "The allowance was made for dust," he said, "not cigarette smoke."

The substance which figured so prominently in Mrs. Johnson's compensation claim was now off the hook entirely.

A Message from Sweden

It might have gone on like this forever, with authorities everywhere throwing out tobacco-based claims as fast as they came in, but for a breakthrough in Sweden. In 1981 a nonsmoking woman filed a claim for workers' compensation after contracting a type of lung cancer normally found only in smokers. She blamed her condition on nine years of exposure to smoke in a drafting office and asked that it be treated as an occupational injury.

The bid went through the familiar process of rejection, appeal and counter-appeal before reaching Sweden's Insurance Court of Appeal. Here the key evidence was provided by the country's National Institute of Environmental Medicine, which had been asked to review epidemiological evidence from around the world. Its verdict was that the balance of probabilities favored the conclusion that the woman's lung cancer had been caused by smoke in her workplace.

In a decision that has powerful implications for judicial and regulatory authorities everywhere – and not least for Canadian compensation boards – the court agreed with the balance of probabilities argument. It held that the claimant's lung cancer was indeed an occupational injury entitling her to 100 per cent compensation. By this time, unfortunately, the woman was dead. Any benefits accrue to her estate.

The decision does not, of course, constitute a binding precedent in Canada. But courts and tribunals in this country also base decisions on a balance of probabilities, so the arguments which convinced the Swedish court should also be persuasive here. The next time a Murdeena Johnson demands compensation based on tobacco smoke, it will be harder for the authorities to turn the claim to dust.

REFUSING TO HIRE SMOKERS

Although companies all over the United States and some in Canada have made a policy of not hiring smokers, the question continues to be asked: Is this a form of illegal discrimination?

The simple answer is that it's not. Lewis Eisen, a Toronto lawyer, points out that "human rights legislation in Canada is based on specific prohibitions, and there is nothing in any provincial or federal legislation which expressly prohibits discrimination based on smoking." [140]

It would be surprising if there were. Although Canadian employers are prohibited under human rights legislation to discriminate on the basis of such things as sex, religion or race, they may – and routinely do – make hiring choices based on what might be termed acquired personal characteristics. No one would question an employer's right to refuse to hire someone noted for quarrelsome behavior, or with a record of problems related to other forms of drug addiction. The employer has an equal right to turn thumbs down on someone who will fill the air with toxic fumes and litter the workplace with ashes.

This is the position taken by the Equal Employment Opportunity Commission in the United States [141] and by such employers as Radar Electric's Warren McPherson in Seattle.

"We started a policy of not hiring people who smoked and this is still the policy at Radar today," says Mr. McPherson. "I am continually asked if this is legal and the answer is inarguably yes. I am always surprised by this question because I am sure that within my lifetime I will see an employer successfully sued and punished severely financially for allowing and perhaps encouraging personnel to smoke, who then become sick or ill.

"I see little difference between an employer's lack of concern for the safety of his employees in regard to smoking as I would if they showed complete disregard of employees with regard to chemicals, asbestos, etc." [142]

9

TAKING ACTION IN THE WORKPLACE

"Because nonsmokers have no option but to be in the workplace, and because this is where they experience their greatest lifetime exposure to second-hand smoke, nonsmoking must be re-established as the workplace norm."
— D.T. Wigle, Bureau of Epidemiology, Laboratory Centre for Disease Control, Health and Welfare Canada. [143]

Many older Canadians can remember a day when people simply didn't smoke at work. It had nothing to do with legislation, for there was none. It had nothing to do with health considerations, because the dangers were little recognized. It was simply that employers didn't like it. They didn't want employees taking time out to smoke when they should be working...smoking was messy and it fouled the air...it didn't "look good" for employees to hang around with cigarettes dangling from their mouths.

As paternalism waned in the workplace, smoking gained ground as an expression of employee independence. Eventually, it became the norm; and the result, while being a gain of sorts for individuality, has been exactly the kind of workplace the old-time bosses had tried to avoid. Time is wasted on the mechanics of smoking...workplaces are littered with dirty ashtrays ...employees communicate with one another and with customers amid clouds of smoke. And the added consequence, which didn't occur to the old-time bosses, is that the workplace has become a distinctly unhealthy environment. It has literally become a smoke trap – the place where nonsmokers suffer their greatest lifetime exposure to the contaminants in second-hand smoke.

A New Mood

But there is a new mood discernible in the workplace. As nonsmokers learn more about the dangers of second-hand smoke they are starting to speak up and to demand changes. Smokers themselves are becoming less self-assertive as they begin to perceive the consequences of their actions. Surveys have shown that 75 to 90 percent would quit if they could, and still other surveys have shown that smokers frequently welcome workplace restrictions as a means of reducing their consumption. Although they may argue for their "rights" as vigorously as ever, many smokers are privately aware that they are on the wrong side of the issue and are more ready than ever before to accept changes.

In many companies, as we have seen, smoking policies have been introduced on the initiative of management. In other situations, all it might take for management to make a decision might be an appeal from nonsmoking employees. However, many employers are nervous about the smoking issue and prefer to avoid it if they can. In such cases, nonsmokers have to be prepared to pursue the matter.

What You Can Do

If you are a nonsmoker who has decided it's time for action on the second-hand smoke problem, here are the main avenues open to you:

1. Alone or in co-operation with other nonsmokers, you can seek to persuade management to implement a smoking policy in the interests of a healthier and more productive workplace.

2. You can enlist the help of your union in making your case. If your contract has a Health and Safety clause, you may be able to launch a grievance.

3. You can seek relief through a provincial or federal regulatory agency.

4. Alone or in co-operation with other nonsmokers, you may ask a court to order your employer to provide safe, healthy working conditions.

Get It In Writing

Whichever path you choose, start a comprehensive file. At some point you may be required to document all your efforts to obtain relief from second-hand smoke. Communications with employers, union officials, doctors or outside agencies should be in writing, and wherever possible you should confirm oral communications by memo. You should also set up a diary to record events and conversations as well as to make sure that undertakings are carried out when promised. This systematic approach will show management that you know what you are doing and are determined to see it through.

A WORKPLACE CAMPAIGN

In all your efforts to solve the smoke problem in your workplace, a guiding principle should be to seek co-operation rather than confrontation. Before doing anything else, try to persuade your employer to take meaningful action on the smoke problem. Only if this approach fails should you consider further measures. And, if it does come to that, you'll be in a better moral and legal position to demand your rights – even to the point of confrontation – if you can show that you have already done everything possible to achieve your objectives through regular workplace channels.

As a first step, write a letter to management explaining that you are worried about your health. Show why the health risk is not eliminated by standard ventilation, special air cleaners, or half-measures such as isolating or segregating employees. Explain that the only way the company can fulfill its legal obligation to provide you with healthy working conditions is by prohibiting smoking in the workplace, or by restricting it to separately ventilated lounges. Request these measures, respectfully but firmly.

If your request produces no satisfactory result, consider group action. The prospects of organizing a successful clean indoor air campaign are probably much better than you realize – starting with the fact that, if yours is a typical workplace, you probably have the numbers on your side. Consider the following:

- As we have pointed out, only 35 to 36 per cent of Canadian adults are smokers. Put another way, nonsmoking adults outnumber smokers by nearly three to one – making them part of a healthy majority in every sense of the term. [144]

- We also know that most nonsmokers find second-hand smoke distasteful and physically bothersome. The Shephard and Labarre study involving 440 Canadian nonsmokers, cited earlier, found only 11.6 per cent who said smoke didn't bother them. A resounding 88.4 per cent considered second-hand smoke objectionable, and fully 83.6 per cent reported adverse physical reactions ranging from stinging eyes (the most common symptom) to headaches and nausea. **Only 16.4 per cent said they experienced no physical reactions.** [145]

- The same researchers also asked over 1,000 Torontonians about specific situations in which second-hand smoke was annoying to them, and 52.5 per cent named offices. What makes this figure especially interesting is that nearly half the people who answered the question were themselves smokers. [146] "Most nonsmokers complain of either annoyance or health effects from such smoke concentrations," the report notes. "It could be argued that this is merely an irrational response on the part of the nonsmoker, but the rather equal perception of the nuisance by the smoker and the nonsmoker is a strong argument against such a possibility." [147]

- In the first section of this manual, we cited a Baltimore study involving 10,000 nonsmoking employees of the U.S. government. Here are some of the findings:
  - More than half reported that second-hand smoke impaired their working efficiency.
  - 36 per cent said they were forced to leave their work stations to avoid breathing second-hand smoke.
  - 10 per cent reported allergic reactions, and 3 per cent complained that second-hand smoke was aggravating a heart condition.
  - Nearly 25 per cent expressed feelings of hostility towards both smokers and management over the second-hand smoke problem. [148]

It's worth bearing in mind that these studies were carried out several years ago. Nonsmokers have become much more sensitive to the second-hand smoke problem since then, and much more ready to object. If those surveys were repeated today, we can be sure they would reveal overwhelming support for action to clear the workplace air.

The Numbers Trap

At this point we offer a warning. While it should be reassuring to you as a nonsmoker to know that you are part of the healthy majority, and while that fact may provide valuable leverage in your campaign to control smoking in your workplace, be careful not to fall into the numbers trap. It can lead to head-counting, and nonsmokers can't be sure they will be a majority in each and every situation. In the end, the case for controlling smoking in the workplace does not rest on how many smoke and how many don't; it rests on the right of every single individual to breathable air and safe, healthy working conditions.

This fundamental principle has been admirably recognized in some of the workplace regulations that have been enacted in California. They provide that, in the event of a complaint about second-hand smoke from a non-smoker, the employer must resolve the problem to the satisfaction of the nonsmoker even if the nonsmoker is alone in a roomful of smokers.

Undemocratic? On the contrary, it is the very essence of enlightened democracy to entrench the rights of individuals and minorities against abuse by majorities. That is what the Canadian Charter of Rights is all about; and the principle that the right to safe, breathable air at work is fundamental and unabridgeable is what this manual is all about.

ORGANIZING

Decide, first, if you are the best person to get a clean air campaign rolling. If you are a natural leader, go ahead and good luck to you. If you aren't, try and find a leader among your fellow nonsmokers. You might want to form a committee of the most concerned nonsmokers and start sharing tasks. Because there will almost surely be opposition, some of it irrational, make sure your organizers and spokesmen are employees in good standing; avoid aligning yourself with known malcontents. Bear in mind that it may require work, perseverance, patience, commitment and perhaps even some courage.

To be truly effective, you and your fellow nonsmokers should make it your business to become experts on the smoking and health issue, and especially the second-hand smoke issue. This manual provides a good start. Commit key pieces of information to memory, as well as some of the more important arguments. And if at times it seems you have taken on quite a load, remember that you are protecting an irreplaceable gift – your health – as well as protecting your livelihood.

The Educational Phase

As you start your organizing efforts, you'll probably find that many nonsmokers in your workplace will be grateful that someone is at last speaking up and will be only too glad to join you. But be prepared to discover that some nonsmokers may actually align themselves with smokers. There can be a number of reasons for this. They may simply not understand that second-hand smoke is harmful to nonsmokers and may feel that you are fussing over nothing. They may be fearful of annoying smokers, especially if smokers are in supervisory or management positions. They may be afraid of becoming identified as troublemakers. Or they may refuse to join you out of a misconceived liberalism which holds that smokers have the same rights as nonsmokers.

The way to convince such people that it's time to do something about second-hand smoke is the same way you convinced yourself – with the facts. Explain the issue and give them some of the literature that's available from health agencies and nonsmokers' rights groups. A nonsmoker who thinks there's nothing wrong with a bit of smoke in the workplace will think differently when confronted with studies showing evidence of lung impairment and disease in otherwise healthy nonsmokers.

Explain to waverers that, by refusing to help, they are in effect voting for a polluted workplace. Talk to nonsmokers about their rights, and about all the possibilities for relief that are being opened up by new legislation. The more people know about the issue, the more likely they are to want to join you.

As for those employees who are worried by the prospect of confrontation, they should be reminded of the stakes – for the cost of silence is lifelong exposure to a workplace hazard. When you talk to those who see themselves as liberals on this issue, tell them that in their attempts to be "fair" to smokers, they are being more than unfair to others. They are not defending a right to smoke, for no one denies that right; the workplace liberal is defending a right to smoke **at will**, which is nothing less than a licence to pollute.

Once you have established a basic support group among fellow nonsmokers, consider extending your educational efforts to the workplace as a whole. If your company has a medical department, ask the staff to support your workplace campaign and get their help in obtaining educational material. Place literature where other employees can see it. Tack brochures on employee bulletin boards. Write letters and articles for your staff newsletter. Raise your concerns at meetings. Explain your concerns to smokers, showing them that they, too, will benefit from clean workplace air. Make the point that a smoking policy will help those who want to control their own smoking.

Since you are dealing with an issue where emotions frequently play a greater role than reason, proceed with as much patience and good humor as possible. There is no need to harangue or adopt a belligerent attitude when the facts speak so loudly for themselves.

Getting the Ammunition

Where basic working conditions are concerned, employers tend to be nervous about change. Your workplace campaign has to make it clear to management that change is both reasonable and necessary, that the issue is well and truly raised, and that it will not go away.

To show that change is necessary you are going to have to develop hard evidence to document the extent of the second-hand smoke problem in your workplace. A survey is a good way to start. You might want to suggest setting up a committee made up of nonsmokers, smokers and management to develop a questionnaire and supervise its distribution. (Make sure the results are made available to your joint committee, not just to management alone.) But the key point is that a survey of this kind should be undertaken only after you have completed the educational phase of your workplace campaign. The more your fellow employees know about the issue when they answer your questionnaire, the more rational and supportive their responses are bound to be. Here are some of the things you might want to find out:

- How many smokers, nonsmokers?

- Where possible, individual cigarette consumption.

- How many are bothered by second-hand tobacco smoke? Nature and strength of complaint. (Make sure you ask smokers as well as nonsmokers.)

- How many have physical reactions to smoke? You might want to provide a check list of reactions such as stinging eyes, nausea, headache, dizziness, wheezing, blocked nose, running nose, sinusitis, phlegm etc.

- How many have medical complaints related to second-hand smoke? At a later stage, such individuals may be asked to strengthen their case with written confirmation from their doctors.

- How many have health conditions that may be aggravated by second-hand smoke, such as heart disease, respiratory disease, allergies etc.? Again, confirmation may be sought later.

- Smoker/nonsmoker distribution in particular work areas.

- Special problems: e.g., a single nonsmoker surrounded by smokers; tensions between particular smokers and nonsmokers; tensions involving employees and managers; poorly ventilated areas.

- Does the presence of tobacco smoke interfere with physical well-being, energy level, productivity? Does it produce a need to get away from the work area for a breath of air? Do smoke-related symptoms (e.g., nasal congestion) interfere with sleep at night?

- Have employees complained to smokers and/or management about tobacco pollution? Results.

- General comments on the second-hand smoke problem.

- How many would welcome a smoking policy?

A No-Lose Strategy

If management doesn't want to co-operate at this stage, or if you decide it's best to gather your ammunition without tipping your hand, you may decide not to circulate a questionnaire. What you can do in this case is conduct an informal, verbal survey of your fellow employees, asking as many questions as possible and noting the answers in your own records.

Broadly based surveys in Canada and the United States have shown that most people object to second-hand smoke and that most approve of smoking curbs. If your workplace is at all typical, the results of your own survey should show similar support for a good, strong smoking policy. But remember – and this is the beauty of your position as a nonsmoker – you can't lose no matter how your survey turns out; for, as we have just pointed out, health is not a numbers game. Even if no one in your workplace supported you, you would still have every moral and legal right to demand the removal of a proven hazardous substance from the workplace air. If a few supported you, your case would be that much stronger. With a majority behind you, your survey becomes a powerful weapon. And if even a few smokers added their support – which is not unlikely – that would put you in an even better position. When it comes to cleaning up your workplace air, numbers can't stop you; they can only help.

More Ammunition

Based on the information produced by your survey, you might want to document special problems with diagrams of particular workplace layouts indicating the placement of fans, ducts, windows etc. Where a nonsmoker is surrounded by smokers, it might help to spell out the problem on a floor plan. Don't neglect anecdotal material. It can be very persuasive to give examples of individual problems together with quoted comments by those involved, if necessary omitting names. Putting this kind of documentary material together strengthens your case and makes the added point that you and other nonsmokers are serious and determined.

MAKING A PRESENTATION TO MANAGEMENT

By now you should be ready to prepare a formal written presentation to management documenting your concerns and setting out your recommendations for cleaning up the air in your workplace. Make it thorough but keep it as concise and businesslike as possible, avoiding emotional or recriminatory language. Make it clear that your proposal is a positive one that is designed to clear up a serious problem in the workplace and provide benefits to all concerned: management as well as employees, smokers as well as nonsmokers.

Start by making the point that you're not objecting merely to a nuisance. Stress that tobacco smoke has been proved to cause disease and disability among nonsmokers. When you cite medical findings, don't use this manual as your only authority; for added credibility, name the original sources identified in the notes. Your survey results will also allow you to document specific smoke-related health problems in your own workplace.

Show that tobacco smoke contains toxic substances, including potent carcinogens, that are not removed by ventilation systems – and are, in fact, distributed by them. Explain that the courts and other authorities have concluded that tobacco smoke is a workplace hazard, that employees have a basic right to clean air, and that there is no countervailing right to indulge in a practice that pollutes the air. You might also want to show how North American courts and regulatory agencies are beginning to find employers liable for the health consequences of workplace smoking. And don't neglect what could turn out to be a powerful argument in your employer's eyes: the economic gains to be made by clearing the air.

Finally, based on your survey results, you might decide to include figures showing the level of support for a smoking policy in your workplace. You might also consider buttressing your presentation with a petition calling for action.

RECOMMENDING A SMOKING POLICY

Once you have explained all the reasons for taking action against second-hand smoke, you will have to recommend a specific policy for your workplace. You can start by examining measures that have been adopted elsewhere in an attempt to deal with the problem, such as the following:

1. Improved ventilation. Special room air cleaners. Desktop ionizers.

2. No smoking in common areas such as elevators, restrooms, lobbies, hallways and stairways, libraries, meeting rooms and computer rooms. No restrictions in work areas.

3. As above. Employees are also supplied with No Smoking notices for their individual desks or work stations.

4. Segregation of smokers and nonsmokers by creating separate sections in the same office or work area.

5. Segregation of smokers and nonsmokers in different rooms or partitioned areas.

6. No smoking in the workplace except in designated smoking areas.

7. No smoking in the workplace except in enclosed, separately ventilated

smoking lounges.

8. No smoking in the workplace.

In recommending a policy for *your* workplace, you must stress the point that there are two kinds of second-hand tobacco smoke. One is the visible cloud found in the immediate vicinity of a smoker. The other is dispersed smoke, which in the course of a day comes to permeate the workplace. This dispersed smoke may well be invisible, and nonsmokers who become accustomed to its presence may no longer even smell it. But it, too, is loaded with contaminants. You must explain in your presentation that, if a smoking policy is to protect the health of nonsmokers, it must deal with this dispersed smoke as well as with exposure at close quarters. Now let us examine the various options set out above:

1. As Repace and Lowrey have shown conclusively, neither improved ventilation nor special air cleaning devices are capable of reducing the health risk from the pollutants in second-hand smoke to a level considered acceptable for other environmental hazards.

2 and **3.** These deal only with exposure at close quarters or with occasional exposure; the nonsmoking employee still faces day-long exposure to smoke produced at the next work station or blown over the work station by passing smokers.

4. This option adds some distance but does not address the problem. It has been demonstrated that smoke from burning cigarettes quickly spreads throughout an enclosed indoor space.

5 and **6.** Unless a room or smoking area has a separate exhaust to the outdoors, smoke produced in such places will find its way into the building's general air supply and be distributed throughout the workplace. You might remember the study cited in an earlier section in which researchers concluded that it takes only one or two smokers to contaminate an entire building. [149]

7. This is the first option that involves no health risk to nonsmokers, and separate ventilation of an enclosed smoking lounge is not costly; all it requires is the installation of a fan and an exhaust duct leading to a washroom ventilating system or the outdoors. But the solution has drawbacks, starting with the fact that smoking lounges underscore the down-time involved in smoking. Employers may not mind seeing a person take a smoke break at a work station; but they may well object to seeing that same person leave the area to smoke. The other problem flows from the fact that a major benefit of a smoking policy should be reduced cigarette consumption by smoking employees, and therefore a healthier and more productive work force. That benefit is lost when employees continue to smoke as before. While you may decide to recommend the installation of enclosed, separately ventilated smoking lounges, this should really be considered a fall-back solution.

8. Here, with a total ban on smoking in the workplace, we come to the option that has been instituted with positive results in a number of forward-looking companies. It's the one Boeing is moving towards in the United States and Canada; it's the one that deals with the workplace pollution problem most directly and effectively; and it's the one that provides the greatest returns in terms of employee well-being and productivity.

Why Not Compromise?

It could be argued at this point that segregation, designated smoking areas and similar workplace arrangements are at least an improvement for nonsmokers, and that improvement is often all that can be expected in a world built on compromise. Why should nonsmokers demand complete satisfaction of their complaints?

The problem here is that objecting to indoor pollutants is not like fussing over working arrangements or the color of the office wallpaper. As we have seen, some of the substances in tobacco smoke are so toxic that health authorities have warned there is **no** safe level of exposure. It's hardly a reasonable compromise to tell a nonsmoker that, by sitting on the other side of the room, he or she will get somewhat **less** of the carcinogen NDMA and all the other poisons in tobacco smoke. Deadly substances in the workplace are not the kind of thing people can be, or should be, expected to compromise on.

> *"The most effective control mechanism of all remains source removal."*
> – James Repace, H. Lowrey. [150]

Thus we recommend that, as a final position, you call for a total ban on smoking in your workplace – or, as a fall-back position, for enclosed, separately ventilated smoking lounges. And don't let anyone tell you the proposal is "too radical." **The radical idea is not that people should be prohibited from smoking in the workplace. It is that they should be allowed, during paid working hours, to indulge an addiction which is destructive to themselves and others and which significantly lowers the productivity of the entire work force.** At bottom, it's no more unreasonable to require smokers to do their smoking outside the workplace than it is to require that they do their drinking elsewhere or pursue other personal activities on their own time.

MULTI-OCCUPANCY BUILDINGS

If you happen to be employed by a company that shares space in a building with other companies, you face a special problem. Even if you persuade your employer to adopt an effective smoking policy, the ventilation system in your working area may well be connected to a common system which circulates smoke produced in other parts of the building.

The first thing to be said is that this is no reason to abandon the attempt to clean up the air in your own premises. A company smoking ban will eliminate your exposure to high-density clouds of smoke produced close at hand, and second-hand smoke carried in the ventilation system will be at lower concentrations than smoke produced locally, all of which must be counted as a gain.

Moreover, a good smoking policy in your company could lead to similar action elsewhere in the building. You might ask your company president to talk to the heads of other companies that share your ventilation system. He will be able to explain the hazards of allowing smokers to contaminate the building and show how the problem was solved in your company. As a concerned nonsmoker, you could also talk to nonsmokers in other parts of the building. If you could win a healthier workplace, so can they. Finally, if all else fails, you could consider a formal appeal to the provincial agency responsible for protecting the health of employees (see later sections). You could explain that, despite your best efforts to protect your health, hazardous substances were still being introduced into your workplace by others.

IMPLEMENTATION BY STAGES

In making your arguments for a ban on workplace smoking, you can point out that you are not asking management to introduce your proposals cold – far from it. Anything as far-reaching as a smoking policy should be implemented only in carefully prepared stages. You might want to suggest proceeding along the following lines:

1. Management announces that it is considering a smoking policy, explaining the concerns that have prompted it to do so. Educational material is made available to the work force.

   At this early stage, your employer might want to consider getting outside help. Consultants with special expertise in the area of workplace smoking can help draft a smoking policy. They can also help to introduce the policy and assist in its implementation. It can be very helpful for management to be able to say that measures are being undertaken on the advice of outside consultants; it has the effect of taking much of the heat off the employer. (The Non-Smokers' Rights Association can make recommendations to companies wishing to engage consultants.)

2. The educational program is intensified. Consultants and outside health authorities hold meetings with employees to discuss the benefits of a nonsmoking policy and to assess various policy alternatives. The aim at this stage is to make the work force clean-air conscious.

3. Management announces the details of a smoking policy and the date on which it will come into force, allowing ample lead time for smoking employees to adjust to the idea and prepare themselves for the new situation. The announcement is accompanied by details of initiatives to ease the adjustment – such as cessation clinics for smokers, monetary incentives etc.

4. The policy comes into effect.

EASING THE WAY

Change of any kind in the workplace tends to produce uneasiness, all the more so when it touches upon addictive behavior. The news that a smoking policy is in the works could well make smokers feel threatened and anxious. Because they will have to curtail what they consider to be a needed activity, and because they will be required to bear the brunt of the adjustment, they may even feel victimized. For these reasons, your recommendations should include measures designed to ease the adjustment for smokers and to remind them that the aim of the new policy is to ensure their well-being as well as that of nonsmokers.

Ask your employer to consider making a smoking cessation program available to employees and, if necessary, to their spouses. Management might also consider paying part of the fee as a way of demonstrating its commitment to employee well-being. You can point out that the costs will be recouped, and more, by reductions in absenteeism and by heightened productivity.

At the same time it's good psychology for smoking employees to have their own financial stake in a cessation program. One possibility might be for management and employees each to pay half, say. Management could provide a valuable added incentive by promising to refund the employees' contribution to those who stay off cigarettes for a year. That's what Johns-Manville of Toronto did when it went to a smoking ban. After employees paid $300 each for a cessation course, the company refunded the money to them in quarterly payments as long as they remained nonsmokers. (It should be noted, by the way, that there's no need for high-cost commercial cessation programs. A study of the literature indicates that they produce no better results than lower-cost programs offered by health agencies and hospitals.) Once again, the point should be made that management's outlay is to be regarded not as a cost but as a self-interested investment in an organization's most important resource – its people.

Employees can also be encouraged to quit with the offer of cold cash. Merle Norman Cosmetics (Canada) Ltd. offered a $40 bonus to quitters when it became smoke-free. [151] One Los Angeles computer company pays $500 for each quitter. [152] That was also the sum paid to office staff by Les Industries du Hockey of Drummondville, Québec, when it instituted a smoking ban in the mid-1970s. It also offered to pay memberships at a health club. According to the magazine *Worklife:* "All of the 17 office staff earned the reward and nearly all joined the health club. Management says the policy had a dramatic effect in cutting absenteeism and keeping the work environment clean."

The company's subsequent experience provides a fascinating glimpse of what can happen when a workplace becomes hooked on clean air. Les Industries has since been taken over by a European holding company and now goes under the name Amer Sports International. The new management dropped the non-smoking policy – but the employees, on their own initiative, have maintained it. Today not a single office worker is a smoker and the company's 150 factory workers do not smoke on the job. Says a staff member: "Smoking just isn't a problem any more. A number of us quit when the nonsmoking policy was introduced – we all quit on the same day – and there just aren't any smokers in the office any more. Sometimes salesmen come in with cigarettes, but they always chuck them as soon as they see the No Smoking sign on the office door." [153]

Paying smokers to quit polluting the workplace seems to work. If there's a drawback to the idea, it lies in the fact that it rewards people for not doing something they shouldn't have been doing in the first place. If bonuses are to be paid, it is probably a much better idea to pay them to **non**smokers; smokers would then be invited to earn the bonus by becoming nonsmokers themselves. That's how one Alabama bank approaches it, paying a $20 monthly bonus to nonsmoking staff. Reports the prestigious *Christian Science Monitor:* "This financial windfall for nonsmokers has cut the number of smokers to less than 15 out of 150 employees and created cleaner offices." [154]

AN INTERIM POLICY

No matter how strong your presentation, how unassailable your arguments, you might find your employers nervous about implementing what to them appears to be a radical change in working conditions. If you should run into such an obstacle, you could suggest moving ahead in two stages. There could be an interim period in which smoking was limited, allowing smokers to get used to the idea that smoking is no longer something that can be done without regard for others. Then your company could move to a total ban.

This should only be a last-ditch proposal in a situation where nothing else will work, for it holds the danger that an interim policy will become a permanent compromise. In setting out such an alternative (which should not, of course, be included in your original presentation), you should remind your employer that this is a half-measure which allows a hazardous practice to continue. If an interim policy is to be implemented, it must be of fixed duration.

The purpose of an interim smoking policy is not to stall but to prepare the work force for a fully effective policy. Obviously, it can only do this if it works, and you should be prepared for the fact that there will be some in the workplace who will not want it to work. The collapse of an interim policy would be held up as proof that the whole idea is impractical and given as a reason for going back to a smoke-filled workplace. As non-smokers, you would have to do your part to ensure that the policy didn't collapse through neglect or obstruction. If smokers ignored the rules, you would have to remind them. If they persisted, you would have to inform management. Remember, the health of everyone in the workplace would be at stake.

A SMOKE-FREE WORKPLACE

You can end your proposal to management on a powerfully positive note, assuring your employer that the experience of other companies has shown a smoke-free workplace to be healthier, happier, more productive and more profitable. Here is how Prof. Weis portrays the benefits:

"An employer who implements a two-pronged approach that both

(a) bans smoking from work premises or restricts it to specially designated, isolated smoking lounges, and

(b) restricts hiring to applicants who either profess to be nonsmokers, or who agree to be nonsmokers during working hours,

will, in the fifth year of the policy,

(a) enjoy real cost savings measurable in thousands of dollars every year for **every** smoker who was on the payroll prior to policy implementation, and

(b) be irreversibly committed to sustaining that policy because of its impact on costs and employee morale." [155]

GO FOR THE TOP

When your presentation is as good as you can make it, ask for a meeting with top management. Don't go to middle-management with your proposals if you can avoid it. People at that level may be nervous about passing your ideas up the ladder and may wish to water them down before doing so. Here is what the Dartnell Institute of Business Research learned in a survey: "In companies contacted, responsibility for developing a smoking policy was assumed by the president in 43 per cent, followed by the vice president, general or office manager, personnel director and controller." And here is something else Dartnell learned: 76 per cent of Chief Executive Officers did not smoke! [156]

Arrange a top-level meeting, then, and take supporters with you. Try to make your delegation broadly representative without making it so large as to be unwieldy or distracting. As well as including fellow nonsmokers, consider inviting someone to represent any smokers who have endorsed your aims. If you have won allies in the medical department or at any level of management, ask them to accompany you. You might also want to invite a physician or other health authority to endorse your proposals. If one of your supporters is a persuasive speaker, you might want to accompany your written proposals with an oral presentation. But if you're not confident on this point, play it safe and stick with what you've written. Whatever you do, arrange your presentation in such a way that no one can be in any doubt about the importance of the occasion.

10

GOING IT ALONE

Organizing a workplace campaign might not always be possible or practical. In some situations, a nonsmoker might not have access to other employees. In industries with little job security, fellow employees might be frightened about asserting their rights. Or there might be a health problem that requires immediate relief from ambient tobacco smoke. In such cases, the nonsmoker may have to go it alone. And here we return to a point made earlier: health isn't a numbers game. The right to breathe clean, safe air is absolute. It doesn't depend on whether nonsmokers can outvote smokers in any given situation. Even if you are a single nonsmoker among many smokers, you have the right to demand a smoke-free environment. In the case of SHIMP vs. NEW JERSEY BELL, cited in an earlier section, Donna Shimp obtained a court injunction that forced the utility to declare her entire building a No Smoking area. A lone individual took on a corporation with huge resources, and won.

For the lone nonsmoker seeking relief from tobacco smoke, many of the principles are the same as for those who go the organizational route:

1. **Become well informed.** Don't leave your health to the experts. Read everything you can find on the subject.

2. **Keep a file.** Get all communications in writing. Record events and conversations. Keep track of dates so you can be sure that you keep your promises and others keep theirs.

3. **Try reason and persuasion first.** Go through established workplace channels, starting with your immediate supervisor and working upward. Going straight to the top is recommended only when nonsmokers have organized and prepared a formal presentation, or when special circumstances exist which permit you to short-circuit regular channels.

4. **Proceed with as much patience and good humor as you can muster.** Don't create opposition needlessly, and remember that a smile can often smooth the way where other means fail.

5. **Seek allies.** Try to find key members of management or union officials who are sympathetic to your views or who are open to persuasion. Needless to say, your chances of finding support are better if you

begin your search among nonsmokers. When you do find well-placed allies, work through them as much as possible. Ask them to pass along your views and requests together with recommendations of their own.

If your company has a full-fledged medical department, try to get the staff on your side. But don't count on automatic support. Some medical personnel don't know as much about the hazards of second-hand smoke as they should. Others could be caught in a bind between their duty to safeguard the health of employees and what they might see as their duty to management to head off or avoid contentious issues. And some medical personnel, of course, are smokers themselves.

If you run into problems in this area, see if you can persuade your medical staff that their first obligation is to good health. Talk to them about your concerns, and make sure they're aware of the latest medical findings on the dangers of second-hand smoke to nonsmokers. It's all worth the effort, for medical personnel can be crucial allies.

You will also need the unreserved support of your own doctor. He or she must be prepared to back you in any representations you make to your employers, and must even be prepared to provide evidence on your behalf if things reach the point of litigation. If your doctor is not whole-heartedly on your side in this vital health matter, shop around and find one who will be.

6. **Gather your ammunition.** Make a written analysis of your particular situation. How many smoke in your area? How much do they smoke? Have you complained to smokers or management? If so, what was the reaction?

   Make a diagram showing your own work station in relation to smokers and to ducts, windows, doors and so forth. Indicate whether the presence of ambient smoke has an effect on your productivity. Does it make you drowsy? Does it force you to leave your work station? Have you ever stayed home because of a smoke-related complaint? Does your exposure at work interfere with your sleep at night?

   List any physical reactions you may have to tobacco smoke, indicating the frequency of the reactions, time of day, etc. Note any complaints you may have made to the company medical department or your own doctor. Obtain written verification of any medical visits.

   But be careful to avoid the "allergy" trap. People who experience physical reactions to tobacco smoke may take this as evidence of an allergy and then ask for special consideration on this account. The fact is that true tobacco allergy is an uncommon condition. Most people who react adversely to second-hand smoke do so for the very good reason that it is a noxious substance; their bodies are simply trying to defend themselves.

   When nonsmokers ask for relief on the grounds of allergy, they shift responsibility for the problem to themselves. They invite their employer to conclude that it is not second-hand smoke which is at the root of the trouble, but their allergic condition. In most cases, nonsmokers would do well to drop the term from their vocabularies. When voicing their concerns about indoor air quality, they should make it clear that they are the concerns of healthy people caught in a decidedly unhealthy situation.

Of course, if you do happen to have a medically diagnosed tobacco allergy which poses a serious and immediate health problem, this must be taken into account in your representations to your employer. So must other pre-existing health conditions which can be aggravated by tobacco smoke, such as heart or respiratory disease. If you have such a condition, get a letter to this effect from your doctor. Ask him or her to back your request for early and effective relief from the discomfort and risk of workplace smoke.

7. **Make a written presentation to management.** Include all your personal ammunition. Cite medical and scientific evidence relating to the dangers of second-hand smoke to nonsmokers, and note the sources. You would also do well to point out that there is a growing body of legal precedent and opinion which holds employers liable for smoke-induced illness and disability. At this point, however, we would caution you not to suggest that you are considering legal action, even if that is in your mind. Remember, we are still in the stage of reason and persuasion.

In your presentation, explain that nothing less will do than a smoke-free working environment. Use the information in this manual to show that establishing physical distance between smokers and nonsmokers may relieve immediate discomfort in some cases but does little to reduce the long-term health risk. Don't accept largely useless desktop gimmicks like personal ion generators, air filters, fans or so-called smokeless ashtrays.

If your employer complains that accommodating you creates a problem, point out that you are not the cause of the problem; it's caused by the introduction into the workplace of substances that don't belong there.

8. **Don't accept a penalty.** You have every right to refuse if your employer offers a solution that involves demotion, a loss of pay or responsibility, reduced career opportunities, or a change of location requiring unacceptable travel. Stress the point that a problem must be solved by addressing the cause, not by penalizing the victim.

9. **Exhaust all possibilities of remedy.** Do everything you can to obtain relief through regular workplace channels. If nothing works and you are forced to seek relief by other means, you will be able to show you are not a hot-head or a crank but a reasonable person with a reasonable demand.

10. **Hang in. Even if nothing comes of your best efforts to obtain relief, don't quit your job. You're in a much better position to take your**

case to governmental regulatory agencies if you are still an employee. If you feel the situation is urgent and you must stay out of the workplace because tobacco smoke is aggravating a medical condition or because it has reached totally unacceptable concentrations, make it clear to management beforehand and in writing that you are not resigning. Explain with regret that you are being forced to stay home for health reasons. If possible, include a doctor's letter or explain that you'll be obtaining one. Make it clear that you fully intend to return to work as soon as circumstances permit. If practical, offer to do work at home.

11

BEYOND THE WORKPLACE

Reason and persuasion don't always work. Even the best-prepared presentation can be rejected. Your union may run into a brick wall. You may have a management that simply doesn't want to budge. What do you do if you have gone through all the proper workplace channels and nothing has helped? What you **don't** do is give up. You look elsewhere for assistance.

At this point, or perhaps even earlier, you should consider retaining a lawyer. The timing should depend on how well you are faring on your own. The more you can accomplish without assuming the expense of counsel, and without introducing the adversarial note that hiring a lawyer may involve, the better for all concerned. But when you start considering remedies outside the workplace, experienced advice can be valuable and in some cases absolutely necessary.

If you reach such a point, look for a lawyer who is sympathetic to your problem – preferably one who has shown an interest in the second-hand smoke problem or who has experience with environmental and/or public interest issues. Referrals can be obtained by asking around. You can also find the right kind of lawyer by consulting a newspaper clipping file and finding out who has handled similar cases. And don't be afraid to interview two or three lawyers before settling on one who suits your purposes. Avoid lawyers who simply enjoy a good fight. For this issue you need one who is a skilled and persuasive negotiator, who is imaginative and capable of picking a path through untried areas of law.

HELP FROM GOVERNMENT

The most obvious place to seek assistance outside the workplace is from provincial and federal regulatory agencies charged with administering health and safety legislation. We must enter a preliminary caution, however. When Canada's health and safety legislation was originally drafted, the intention was to protect workers against high-level industrial hazards – harsh chemicals, coke oven emissions, garage fumes and so forth. Tobacco smoke was not considered an important source of workplace pollution and is not named anywhere in the legislation.

Still, this should not discourage nonsmokers from seeking relief under such legislation. Even if tobacco smoke is not named, the wording of the various health and safety statutes across Canada leaves ample room for its inclusion alongside traditionally recognized workplace hazards. Consider, for example, how a hazard is defined in Ontario's Health Protection and Promotion Act:

"Health hazard means,
i. a condition of a premises,
ii. a substance, thing, plant or animal other than man, or
iii. a solid, liquid, gas or combination of any of them,

that has or that is likely to have an adverse effect on the health of any person."

Given that wording, and given the medical evidence that is piling up on all sides, it's hard to see how anyone could argue that second-hand smoke is **not** a health hazard within the meaning of the Health Protection and Promotion Act, or of most of the health and safety legislation in Canada.

It should also be noted that, while tobacco smoke is not named in any legislation, some of its constituents are. They are found in the air quality standards published by the American Conference of Governmental Industrial Hygienists, and these standards have the weight of law in most Canadian jurisdictions. They are embodied in the Canada Labor Code and in health and safety statutes in Newfoundland, New Brunswick, Nova Scotia and the Northwest Territories. In four provinces – British Columbia, Alberta, Saskatchewan and Québec – the ACGIH standards are used as the basis for their own regulations. Even where they don't appear in legislation, as in Ontario and Manitoba, they serve as guidelines.

The importance of all this for nonsmokers is that the ACGIH guidelines set Threshold Limit Values for several substances found in tobacco smoke. Where the TLVs are embodied in law, it means that these substances are subject to legally enforceable ceilings. And, as we saw in an earlier section, two of them – 2-Naphthylamine and 4-Aminobiphenyl – have actually been assigned a TLV of Zero, which means they are not to be tolerated in any amount.

The logic is inescapable: If two of the constituents of tobacco smoke are not to be tolerated in the workplace – according to statutory air quality standards in most Canadian jursidictions – then the smoke itself cannot be tolerated. This is the kind of argument that is available to nonsmokers who choose to seek relief by appeal to health and safety legislation. It remains for nonsmokers to take their complaints to provincial and federal regulatory agencies and to insist that these agencies live up to their duty to protect employees from workplace hazards, **whatever the source.**

A BREAKTHROUGH FOR NONSMOKERS

An example of what can be accomplished by a single determined nonsmoker is provided by the case of Peter Wilson, a former clerk with Health and Welfare Canada in Toronto. As a steward for the Public

Service Alliance, which is the federal civil service union, he had been asked to help a female employee who became ill and was forced to miss work because of tobacco smoke in her workplace.

At Wilson's urging, employees in the section agreed to a rearrangement of desks that to some extent would have diminished the impact of the smoke. But it was the same old story: The office manager didn't want to set a precedent. Ex-smoker Wilson therefore launched a grievance on his own behalf, demanding that smoking be restricted to a separately ventilated area. The grievance went all the way to the Deputy Minister before it was finally rejected. The reason, he was told, was that Health and Welfare Canada was preparing a departmental smoking policy that would address his concerns.

Convinced it would be years before any such relief was forthcoming, he saw no reason why he and other nonsmokers should have to keep breathing noxious fumes in the meantime. With full union backing, Wilson launched a second grievance, this one containing a novel twist. He charged that Health and Welfare Canada was in violation of the collective agreement by condoning a dangerous substance in the workplace.

Raising the Stakes

He based his case on the Dangerous Substances Safety Standard, which is derived from the Canada Labor Code and is incorporated in all collective agreements between the federal government and its employees. It provides that any substance in the workplace air which is "dangerous to the safety or health of any person who is exposed to it" must not exceed the Threshold Limit Values set out in the ACGIH guidelines (see previous section). And, as the grievance pointed out, the guidelines say two of the substances found in tobacco smoke must not be tolerated in any amounts.

Wilson had clearly raised the stakes, for the issue was no longer limited to his personal work space. If his grievance were upheld on the basis of the Dangerous Substances Safety Standard, the federal government could be forced either to ban smoking for its employees all across Canada or to establish separately ventilated areas for smokers.

The grievance was fought all the way to the Public Service Staff Relations Board, where Wilson found himself pitted against the Treasury Board in its role as official federal employer as well as against his immediate employer, Health and Welfare Canada. The government initially took refuge in a legalism, arguing that tobacco smoke is not a dangerous substance within the meaning of the Standard. The reason given was the same as that given by authorities everywhere when confronted by complaints about workplace tobacco smoke: It was maintained that the legislation was not drafted with tobacco smoke in mind.

It's a bizarre contention when you think about it – much like saying that auto theft can be no crime since property laws were drafted before the invention of automobiles. And for once the argument didn't wash. It's not what legislators intend to say that counts, the ajudicator ruled – it's what they actually do say. If tobacco smoke IS demonstrably harmful to nonsmokers, he declared, then the Dangerous Substances Safety Standard clearly applies.

This left the government in the awkward position of arguing, against the weight of scientific and medical opinion, that tobacco smoke is NOT demonstrably dangerous to nonsmokers. It was especially embarrassing for Health and Welfare Canada, which is charged with safeguarding public health and clearly knows better. In fact, two of the five expert witnesses arguing against the government position were its own specialists on problems of tobacco and disease.

As it developed, the government didn't stand a chance. Wilson's star witness was none other than James Repace, the U.S. government scientist whose findings figure so prominently in this book. Of 13 epidemiological studies investigating the relationship between passive smoking and lung cancer, he testified, 12 have found an association.

According to Repace's calculations, smoke concentrations in Wilson's work area produced a cancer risk "100 to 250 times that considered acceptable under standard criteria for environment carcinogens in air, water or food." The only way to reduce the risk to an acceptable level would be "complete physical separation of the grievor from tobacco smoke-contaminated atmospheres or a banning of smoking on the grievor's floor."

'Nonsmokers are Light Smokers'

Dr. Neville Lefcoe, a Canadian specialist in respiratory diseases, said the urine and saliva of nonsmokers in typical working environments contain enough tobacco-related substances to justify placing such individuals in the category of "light smokers." And yes, he said, there is "very good evidence that passive smoke causes lung cancer."

Dr. Donald Wigle, chief of Health and Welfare Canada's Non-Communicable Diseases Division, said there is no question that Canadians get lung cancer from second-hand smoke. The only question is how many.

One of the few light moments at the hearing was provided by another Health and Welfare Canada expert, Neil Collishaw of the Bureau of Tobacco Control. Citing U.S. environmental authorities, he said anyone forced to handle 2-Naphthylamine (which as we have just seen is one of the more powerful carcinogens in tobacco smoke) "should be fully protected with impervious clothing and air-supplied breathing equipment. Also the hands, feet and eyes should be covered."

Observed Mr. Collishaw: "It is not practical to so equip public servants."

The government produced only one expert witness – Theodore Sterling, a professor of computer science at British Columbia's Simon Fraser University. He conceded that cigarettes give off many toxic substances, including carcinogens, but maintained that they are quickly dispersed and diluted in normally ventilated space. With so many poisons in the air, he said, no one can pinpoint the effects of tobacco smoke. He also quarrelled with the methods and results of international studies linking passive smoking and lung cancer.

In the end Dr. Sterling received short shrift from the ajudicator, who noted that the witness once told a U.S. Senate Committee there is no proof tobacco smoke kills even active smokers. On that occasion, the ajudicator observed, Dr. Sterling appeared on behalf of the U.S. Tobacco Institute (he is, in fact, a frequent guest at seminars and meetings funded by the tobacco industry). Finally, it was noted that Dr. Sterling had done no research of his own on the effects of passive smoking. Concluded the ajudicator:

"In my view, Dr. Sterling's testimony, insofar as it is in conflict with the testimony of the other expert witnesses, must give way to that testimony. As Dr. Wigle testified, a conclusion can never be based on one study in epidemiology because of unknown confounding factors. It is important to have a series of studies showing consistent results. Dr. Wigle and Mr. Repace agreed that a body of evidence now exists that shows passive smoking to be a cause of lung cancer."

A Grievance Upheld

In his written judgment (see appendix IX) the ajudicator said:

"I have conducted a careful analysis and review of all of the expert testimony and I have come to the conclusion that, on a balance of probabilities, the evidence presented on behalf of the grievor establishes the existence of a statistically significant co-relation between exposure to passive smoke and an increased incidence of lung cancer.

"As a consequence, I find that passive tobacco smoke is a 'dangerous substance' within the meaning of the Standard." Improved ventilation is no answer, he said. The only way nonsmoking employees can be adequately protected is by restricting smoking to separately ventilated rooms of floors.

The grievance was upheld, although in one sense the outcome was academic. Peter Wilson had by this time left his job and thus no ruling was made with respect to smoke in his former work area. At the time of writing the outcome is momentarily blurred by the government's decision to appeal to the Federal Court of Canada. It should be noted, however, that an appeal can deal only with points of law; the evidence will stand.

None of this, in fact, detracts from the immense significance of the ruling, for this was no ordinary hearing. The ajudicator, Walter Nisbet, is Deputy Chairman of the Public Service Staff Relations Board and possessor of an extensive legal background. His findings were made only after painstaking examination of expert testimony, sophisticated scientific research and critical commentary. So painstaking was his report, which runs to a remarkable 179 pages, that it has been hailed in the press as a landmark which moves Canada a giant step closer to the smoke-free work environment.

"The ajudicator's ruling has a wide-reaching precedential effect," according to Wilson's Ottawa lawyer, Derek Dagger. "The Dangerous Substances Safety Standard, upon which the decision was based, is identical to the dangerous substances section in the Canada Labor Code."

This means the decision will have a bearing on employees of federally regulated industries as well as federal civil servants – in all, some 700,000 people. Similar wording is also found in a great deal of provincial legislation. Furthermore, Mr. Dagger noted, many collective agreements in the private sector contain wording similar to that in federal agreements. Literally millions of Canadians will be able to cite the Peter Wilson decision in their demand for smoke-free workplaces.

And it could well go even further than that, according to Mr. Dagger. If the government goes ahead with its appeal of the ruling, and the ruling is upheld, it will come to have the force of legal precedent. Confronted with a complaint about second-hand tobacco smoke, regulatory authorities will no longer be able to say: "Oh, we have nothing to do with that!"

• • •

For nonsmokers who may be thinking of taking their case to a regulatory agency, the following chart sets out the principal pieces of health and safety legislation under which relief can be sought.

CANADA'S PRINCIPAL HEALTH AND SAFETY LEGISLATION

JURISDICTION	ACT	ADMINISTERING AGENCY
British Columbia	Workers' Compensation Act	Workers' Compensation Board
British Columbia	Factory Act	Ministry of Labor
Alberta	Occupational Health & Safety Act	Alberta Workers' Health, Safety & Compensation
Saskatchewan	Occupational Health & Safety Act	Department of Labor
Manitoba	Workplace Safety & Health Act	Department of Environment and Workplace Safety and Health
Ontario	Occupational Health & Safety Act	Ministry of Labor
Ontario	Health Protection & Promotion Act	Ministry of Health
Québec	Act respecting Occupational Health & Safety	Commission de la Santé et de la Sécurité du Travail
New Brunswick	Occupational Health & Safety Act	Occupational Health and Safety Commission
Nova Scotia	Health Act	Department of Health
Nova Scotia	Construction Safety Act	Department of Labor and Manpower
Nova Scotia	Industrial Safety Act	Department of Labor and Manpower
Prince Edward Island	Workers' Compensation Act	Workers' Compensation Board
Newfoundland	Occupational Health & Safety Act	Department of Labor
Northwest Territories	Safety Ordinance	Department of Justice and Public Service, Yellowknife
Yukon	Workers' Compensation Ordinance	Department of Consumer and Corporate Affairs/Justice
Federal civil servants	(Departmental standards)	Treasury Board, Ottawa
Most employees of federally regulated industries	Canada Labor Code	Labor Canada
All federal employees as of 1986	Canada Labor Code (amended)	Labor Canada

If you want to know more about the health and safety legislation in your province, contact the government department responsible for administering it. You can also get free technical and legal information by contacting the Canadian Centre for Occupational Health and Safety. You may use the centre's toll-free telephone number – 1(800) 263-8276 – or write to the following address:

Canadian Centre for Occupational Health and Safety
250 Main Street East, Hamilton, Ontario L8N 1H6

REFUSING TO WORK

Most Canadian jurisdictions grant employees certain limited rights to refuse to work in the presence of a workplace hazard. Legislation in Alberta and Newfoundland recognizes such a right in situations of "imminent danger." British Columbia and Saskatchewan don't require employees to carry on work which they have reasonable cause to believe would expose them to an undue health or safety hazard.

Similarly, New Brunswick and Quebec allow an individual to refuse work where it is believed the work is a danger to personal safety. Under Ontario's Occupational Health and Safety Act individuals may refuse to work where they believe the physical condition of the workplace is likely to endanger them. The Canada Labor Code, as originally drafted, allowed employees to refuse to work in the presence of "imminent danger" or "a threat of injury to your safety or health which is likely to happen at any moment without warning."

The language makes clear that most of this legislation, like health and safety legislation in general, was designed to protect employees from immediate physical danger, not from the long-term danger presented by exposure to tobacco smoke. And, indeed, judicial and regulatory authorities have so far insisted on this restrictive view.

A Despairing Protest

This is illustrated in the case of Albert Timpauer, a baggage foreman for Air Canada in Toronto. A nonsmoker, Timpauer suffered severe allergic reactions to heavy concentrations of smoke in his workplace. Repeated complaints led to an inspection by Air Canada's manager for employee safety, who reported as follows:

"I have visited the two main areas in question . . . and have found them to be very poorly ventilated, also sorely in need of a clean-up, especially the air filters on the ventilation fans. It is impossible to use those areas without being exposed to significant amounts of cigarette smoke so long as smoking is permitted there . . ."

The official recommended a series of smoking restrictions, and so did Air Canada's director of medical administration. When his employers refused to act, Timpauer walked off the job in a despairing protest. In doing so, he invoked the Canada Labor Code's "imminent danger" clause.

That didn't work either. Timpauer was promptly ordered back to work by a Labor Canada inspector on the grounds that danger from tobacco could not be considered "imminent." He obeyed, but appealed the ruling to the Canada Labor Relations Board.

The board proved unsympathetic and agreed to hear only one of a list of expert witnesses who were prepared to testify on Timpauer's behalf.

In rejecting the appeal, the board explained that "its instinct was to want to help Mr. Timpauer and nonsmokers generally who have trouble putting up with other people's use of the 'weed.' " However, "that help cannot properly come through the invocation of the 'imminent danger' section of the Canada Labor Code." That section was meant only for situations in which "it is probable that something drastic is going to happen almost immediately."

A Revealing Observation

The decision concluded with the revealing observation that "Mr. Timpauer was really asking the board not to adjudicate his particular complaint but in reality to legislate significant social change – which is the job of Parliament, not the prerogative of the Canada Labor Relations Board."

If we read the statement correctly, it contains an interesting confession. In view of the possible social implications, the board seemed to be saying, it would not have ruled in Timpauer's favor no matter what the evidence showed. It was not about to cause waves.

Does that mean nonsmokers must abandon all thought of refusing to work in the presence of tobacco smoke?

Happily, no. For in this area, too, the situation is brightening. The most significant change has been a series of amendments to the Canada Labor Code. Effective in April, 1986, danger is redefined as "any hazard or condition that could reasonably be expected to cause injury or illness to a person exposed thereto before the hazard or condition can be corrected." And it no longer need be "imminent."

However, a proviso has been carried over from the earlier legislation. It says a refusal to work is not justified if the danger is "inherent in the employee's work or is a normal condition of employment" – and here lie the seeds of a debate. While the term "inherent" should raise no problems – smoking is certainly not a necessary part of any production process – some employers may want to argue that it is a "normal condition of employment" if it has been the accepted practice in a workplace.

Faced with this argument, nonsmokers would have to point out that the term surely was never inserted in the legislation to justify the continuation of a practice that has been discovered to be clearly dangerous. For example, an employee could not be required to work in asbestos-laden air on the grounds that this had previously been the norm.

A New Workplace Norm

In truth, there is nothing "normal" about an addictive practice which contaminates the workplace air, which causes health problems for nonsmokers, and which is indulged in by a diminishing minority. Indeed, when we look at the decline in the numbers of smokers it becomes evident that NOT smoking has become the norm. As the trend continues it will be increasingly difficult for anyone to maintain that it should be regarded as the norm in anywhere, including in the workplace.

Martin O'Connell, a former federal labor minister and now head of the Canadian Centre for Occupational Health, said he's not certain how the amended Code will be interpreted. "But personally I wouldn't think it would be an abuse [of the legislation] to refuse to work because of tobacco smoke." [157]

The federal government certainly expects nonsmokers to try. In his report on the Timpauer case, Air Canada's employee safety manager wrote as follows:

"I met with the Labor Canada officer assigned to the case, and he said that at the present time there is no prohibition in the Canada Labor Code against tobacco smoke in the workplace. It is, however, the opinion of Labor Canada that when the new amendments to the Code are proclaimed [as they now have been] . . . nonsmoking employees will invoke Section 35, Refusal to Work, in those areas where smoking is permitted, on the grounds that their health is being adversely affected."

Henry Nur, deputy director of Labor Canada's Occupational Health and Safety Branch, made a similar prediction:

"The [amended] legislation wasn't oriented towards [tobacco smoke] specifically, but certainly if [nonsmokers] think it will serve their case, I expect them to make a trial case of it." [158]

The Code is Liberalized

The new language has certainly liberalized the tone of the Canada Labor Code so far as refusal to work is concerned, and this has potentially broad implications. The Code is directly applicable to 100,000 Canadians in a wide range of federally regulated industries – radio and television, transport and communications, banking, grain handling, nuclear power and so on – as well as to 245,000 federal civil servants and 355,000 employees of some 40 Crown corporations. To this must be added the fact that the Code influences the thinking of legislators in other jurisdictions and those responsible for interpreting health and safety legislation across Canada.

Another encouraging factor has undoubtedly been the decision of the federal ajudicator in the Peter Wilson case, described above. His ruling that tobacco smoke is a dangerous substance in the workplace will make it a great deal easier for employees everywhere to contend that they have a right to refuse to work in smoke-contaminated surroundings. While it may be true that Canada's refusal-to-work legislation was not drafted with nonsmokers in mind, it is becoming daily harder for regulators to exclude them from its protection.

At the same time nonsmokers should be reminded that refusing to work is a major step which should be contemplated only after everything else has failed. The law in this area can be tricky, and employees who fail to follow prescribed procedures can expose themselves to penalty and loss of income. If you are considering this route, you should first consult the appropriate regulatory agency in your jurisdiction and make sure you understand all the requirements of the legislation. Better still, think about consulting a lawyer who specializes in this area of law.

Note: Albert Timpauer appealed the decision of the Canada Labor Relations Board to the Federal Court of Appeal on the grounds that he was denied "natural justice" because of the Board's refusal to hear relevant witnesses. As this book goes to press, the Federal Court of Appeal granted Timpauer his appeal and referred the matter back to the Board. However, with the changes to the Canada Labour Code referred to above now in effect, Timpauer may lodge a new grievance and test the protection provided by the new amendments.

12

GOING THE UNION ROUTE

Unions have so far played little part in the fight for safe workplace air. Some union officials feel they can't take sides on the issue because "our smoking members have rights too." Others, remembering a day when unions fought for the privilege of smoking on the job, see smoking regulations as a step backward.

Albert Timpauer . . .

Albert Timpauer, the Air Canada baggage foreman whose story is told above, ran into this problem when he sought to enlist the International Association of Machinists and Aerospace Workers in his battle for a smoke-free workplace. When he walked off the job and invoked the refusal-to-work clause in the Canada Labor Code, the union refused to back him. Its position was that Air Canada was developing policies on smoking and that a satisfactory solution to Timpauer's problem would "ultimately be achieved."

When he lost his appeal before the Canada Labor Relations Board, Timpauer decided to launch a grievance on the grounds that Air Canada was condoning a dangerous substance in the workplace (the argument was borrowed directly from Peter Wilson, the Health and Welfare Canada clerk whose fight has already been described). Once again Timpauer's union adopted a hands-off attitude. This time it argued that the complaint was not a proper matter for a grievance and should have been taken up with Air Canada's health and safety committee. Timpauer pushed on alone and, and again was met with rejection.

. . . and Peter Wilson

Matters started in much the same way for Peter Wilson, himself. When he launched his first grievance, the Public Service Alliance refused to become involved. It told him, much as the machinists' union first did in Timpauer's case, that the problem was being handled adequately by the employer. As we saw, Wilson launched his grievance anyway and – again like Albert Timpauer – got nowhere.

In launching his second grievance, Wilson decided it was essential to get the PSA behind him. He vigorously lobbied the union, producing studies and statistics to show that the smoke problem was too serious and too pressing to be allowed to drift.

"That was my toughest job, persuading them," he relates. "But I managed it. They came to see the merits of my case and backed me 100 per cent."

This time, the union supplied Wilson with a lawyer and stood by him all the way to the Public Service Staff Relations Board. And this time he won.

The PSA turnabout provides a dramatic illustration of how union leaders are now beginning to see the issue of passive smoking in a more realistic light. Like regulatory officials, like politicians, like the public itself, they are beginning to see that the right to safe, breathable workplace air is paramount, and that no one – union member or not – has a right to jeopardize the health of fellow workers.

If you as a nonsmoker decide to go the union route in your bid for safe workplace air, be prepared to do some selling. Concentrate your first efforts on union stewards and other officials who are nonsmokers. Get other members on your side by explaining your concerns and making literature available to them. Make prepared presentations to your health and safety committee. Waste no opportunity to make the basic point that tobacco smoke in the workplace is as dangerous to the health and well-being of working people as any of the hazards which unions have fought to eliminate in the past.

Remember, the facts are all on your side. All you have to do is get them into the right hands.

GOING TO COURT

If all else fails, you may want to consider the next and final step – taking your employer to court. Needless to say, this decision can only be made in consultation with a lawyer – preferably, as we have said before, one who is sympathetic to your situation and experienced in the areas of environmental and public interest law. If your favorite lawyer is a smoker who works only in real estate, find another one for your present purpose. You need an individual who can recommend a course of action based on legislation in your own province and who can advise you on the current mood of the courts with regard to this kind of action.

The first thing to be said is that we are dealing here with a rather new area of law. The courts have little past experience to go on in deciding questions involving a widespread environmental hazard such as tobacco smoke. This presents nonsmokers and their lawyers with both a challenge and an opportunity to explore various avenues of judicial recourse. When everything is new, there is a high premium on imagination and resourcefulness.

One of the forms of relief that might be sought from the courts is an injunction, or court order, based on the accepted common law principle that an employer is obliged to provide a safe and healthy workplace, free from **unnecessary** hazardous substances. This is what Donna Shimp used to win a smoke-free environment from the Bell Corporation in New Jersey, and at this moment it remains the most promising avenue of relief for non-smoking employees. Here is how Mrs. Shimp's request for an injunction was set out in her complaint before the New Jersey Superior Court:

"WHEREFORE, plaintiff demands judgment:

(1) That defendant, New Jersey Bell Telephone Company, be directed to provide plaintiff with a workplace free from injurious and toxic substances.

(2) Permanently enjoining defendant from affecting plaintiff's rate of pay or conditions of employment as a result of medical conditions caused by or permitted to exist by defendant, New Jersey Bell Telephone Company."

It should be pointed out that Mrs. Shimp was able to obtain the injunction despite the fact that she was a union member. In most U.S. and Canadian jurisdictions, courts tend to take the position that they have no jurisdiction in matters between employees and employers. Union members with grievances are required to seek remedies through union channels, with final recourse to their labor relations boards.

Mrs. Shimp showed that there is a way around this problem. Arguing that regular labor relations channels had failed to provide relief, she persuaded the New Jersey Court to take jurisdiction on common law principles of equity on the basis of the common law right to a safe and healthy workplace. The Shimp case thus stands as an encouraging precedent for any nonsmoker seeking injunctive relief from tobacco smoke.

Conceivably, a nonsmoker could also seek damages from an employer, but here the legal issues are more complex. To begin with, a damage suit normally requires the complainant to show that damage has already been done. But tobacco smoke works slowly, and it takes a long time for symptoms to develop. By the time a nonsmoker was in a position to sue on the basis of demonstrable health damage, his or her health would already be ruined. By that late date, monetary damages would be cold comfort indeed. An even more important problem arises from the fact that non-smokers tend to be exposed to tobacco smoke in a variety of situations. It could be difficult to prove that specific health damage was caused by exposure in a specific place, such as the workplace.

Damages might also be sought on the grounds of economic loss – if, for example, the reluctance of nonsmokers to accept exposure to tobacco smoke caused them to lose opportunities or even to lose their jobs. But we must point out that this kind of remedy, like the injunction, remains relatively untried in cases involving second- hand smoke. At this stage it would be hard to predict the result of an action.

Still, nonsmokers should not be discouraged from going to court when other remedies have failed and they are at the end of their tether. As the medical evidence continues to accumulate, and as the public becomes more sensitive to the rights of nonsmokers to breathe free, we can confidently expect the courts to become ever more receptive to suits against employers who knowingly permit a hazard to exist in the workplace.

The legal route ultimately holds immense promise. When the courts begin to grant injunctions to nonsmoking employees and to award damages to those injured by second-hand smoke, we can be sure the workplace air will clear as if by magic.

13

A WIDER ARENA

> The tobacco problem "is 90 per cent political and only 10 per cent medical."
> — Michael Pertschuk, former U.S. Federal Trade Commissioner, speaking at the Fifth World Conference on Smoking and Health, Winnipeg, 1983. [159]

For nonsmokers who are unable to achieve safe, healthy workplace air in any of the ways we have discussed so far, there is yet another way: It is to work for legislative change.

This is far from being a counsel of despair, for it's been shown in the United States that governments can, and will, act where employers will not. And there is this important difference: While a company smoking policy can improve the situation of those employed by that company, legislated smoking policies can improve the situation of thousands upon thousands of nonsmokers at the stroke of a pen.

"While much is known about the science of cancer," writes Dr. Epstein (see earlier section), "its prevention depends largely, if not exclusively, on political action." [160]

To nonsmokers whose way is blocked in the workplace, we make the following suggestions:

- Write to your provincial legislative member urging a Clean Indoor Air Act along the lines of Minnesota's act (see earlier sections). Stress the need for effective health and safety regulations for nonsmoking employees.

- Write to your member of Parliament demanding federal action on the tobacco issue. Ask for clean indoor air regulations for buildings and transportation under federal jurisdiction. Urge a ban on all tobacco advertising and promotion.

- Write to your aldermen, pointing to the strides made in places like San Francisco and asking for similar municipal legislation.

- Carry the fight into the public arena. Write letters to the editor, and consider joining or supporting organizations that are fighting for the rights of nonsmokers.

THE ROOT OF THE PROBLEM

As a final point we'd like to stress that the call for a ban on tobacco advertising and promotion is no mere academic exercise. The basic thrust of the industry's advertising efforts – more important than flogging Brand "A" or Brand "B" – is to persuade the world that smoking is an acceptable activity wherever it is carried out, including in the workplace. To attack the ads is to attack the second-hand smoke problem at its very root. And there is this bonus: When the advertising and promotion of tobacco are banned altogether – as will inevitably happen – we will have taken a crucial step towards freeing our children and their children from a centuries-old scourge.

"But you can't tell people not to advertise a legal product!" say the tobacco companies and all those publications that thrive on tobacco ads. "What about the freedom of the marketplace?"

The legal-product argument can best be answered with a question: If someone came up with a similar product tomorrow – one that was powerfully addictive and known to cause a wide range of diseases – would it be approved for sale? It wouldn't, of course. If tobacco is legal today, it's only because it became entrenched in the marketplace before anyone really understood its destructive properties and before there were government regulations to exclude harmful products.

A number of societies are now trying to correct their mistake, not by banning tobacco – it's too late for that – but by trying to inhibit its use and sale, and by trying to keep new generations from becoming addicted. Those in the tobacco industry and in publishing who say society can't ban tobacco ads are really saying it can't be allowed to correct its mistake. They are telling us that the "unrivalled tale of illness, disability and death" can have no end. [161]

It **can**, of course, and a ban on tobacco ads will significantly hasten that end. So will pressure by nonsmokers for effective workplace legislation, and pressure in the workplace itself for policies to control and eliminate smoking. It's a many-sided battle which, as we said earlier, requires energy, determination and even courage. But it's worth every bit of it, because what nonsmokers are fighting for is nothing less than the right to breathe.

APPENDIX I

Excerpts from *Smoking and Health in Ontario: A Need For Balance*

A Report of the Task Force on Smoking for the Ontario Council of Health, May 1982

(The Council of Health is an advisory Council for the Ontario Minister of Health. Copies of this excellent 126 page report, probably the major Canadian review of the smoking problem in the last decade, may be obtained from the Ontario Government Bookstore, 880 Bay Street, Toronto, Ontario M7A 1N8. Cost $3.00.)

CHAPTER TWO: THE PROBLEM OF SMOKING

Smoking is a problem because it is a major and preventable cause of ill-health, disability, and premature death. Smoking by adults causes harm to users, harms or irritates others (including the unborn), provides a bad example to children, and complicates the setting of safe levels of air-borne pollutants in industrial plants and elsewhere...

The problems of smoking do not lend themselves to simple solutions. Yet the health consequences of smoking make effective control imperative. The magnitude, seriousness, and multiplicity of health consequences of smoking are clear, and well-documented; the need for concerted action cannot be questioned from a health perspective...

Second-hand smoke can increase health risks. Evidence in this new research area is accumulating rapidly. Cigarette smoking in various everyday environments may give rise to levels of harmful substances (e.g. carbon monoxide, particulates, nicotine) well above those normally found in the absence of cigarette smoke, and often in excess of standards for human exposure. Tobacco smoke aggravates symptoms in nonsmokers with various pre-existing diseases. Parental smoking has adverse effects on otherwise healthy children. Quite brief (10-15 minute) exposure may increase discomfort and the likelihood of eye infection in healthy adults; daily exposure over many years has been shown to impair respiratory function and may increase the likelihood of lung cancer in non-smoking adults. Second-hand smoke is a significant source of annoyance and irritation in both smokers and non-smokers.

● ● ●

RECOMMENDATION 1:
Protection from Passive Smoking

IT IS RECOMMENDED THAT THE GOVERNMENT OF ONTARIO TAKE LEGISLATIVE MEASURES TO ENSURE A UNIFORM STANDARD OF PROTECTION FROM PASSIVE SMOKING IN SPECIFIED PUBLIC PLACES IN ALL JURISDICTIONS OF THE PROVINCE.

IN ADDITION, IT IS RECOMMENDED THAT THE GOVERNMENT ADOPT IMMEDIATELY NON-SMOKING PROVISIONS IN THE PUBLIC AREAS WITHIN ITS OWN BUILDINGS AND FACILITIES.

IT IS ALSO RECOMMENDED THAT THE GOVERNMENT ADOPT POLICIES TO PROHIBIT OR OTHERWISE EFFECTIVELY CONTROL SMOKE IN TRANSIT SYSTEMS WHICH THE GOVERNMENT LICENSES OR SUBSIDIZES.

The rationale for these restrictions on smoking is twofold:

1. The public needs to be protected against the health hazards and discomfort associated with exposure to second-hand smoke.

2. Development of environmental and social supports encouraging non-smoking is fundamental to other recommendations and an effective smoking program.

• • •

RECOMMENDATION 3:
Smoking in the Workplace

THE GOVERNMENT OF ONTARIO SHOULD DEVELOP AND DEMONSTRATE EFFECTIVE STRATEGIES FOR LIMITING SMOKING IN THE WORKPLACE, STARTING WITH THE GOVERNMENT WORK-PLACE, AND SUBSEQUENTLY PROMOTE THE IMPLEMENTATION OF SUCH PROGRAMS IN BUSINESS, COMMERCIAL AND INDUSTRIAL ESTABLISHMENTS.

IT ALSO IS RECOMMENDED THAT THE GOVERNMENT SPECIFICALLY PROVIDE NON-SMOKING EMPLOYEES THE RIGHT BY LAW TO APPLY FOR AND RECEIVE, WITHOUT PREJUDICE, RELIEF FROM EXPOSURE TO SECOND-HAND SMOKE IN THEIR USUAL WORKPLACE.

The Ministry of Health already has developed initiatives to control smoking in the government workplace. The acceptance and success of these measures reflect the shift in social climate which has occurred in recent years. Stronger smoking inititatives now are more likely to be well received.

Limitations on smoking in the workplace serve two ends:

1. The workplace is likely to be a particularly important environment for the development of non-smoking norms.

2. The health consequences of smoking in the workplace are significant and varied.

Surveys in Ontario suggest that perhaps one-third of all employees experience discomfort. A variety of disabling effects may interfere with ability to work. The long term health consequences of sustained exposure may be significant. Finally, in some settings smoking interacts with other occupational factors to increase risk greatly.

THE HEALTH RISKS OF INVOLUNTARY SMOKING

5. Reference to threshold limit values for ambient air quality standards has been useful in the initial assessment of levels of specific substances found under passive smoking conditions. However, these standards were drawn up for different purposes, and may not be appropriate for assessing the long-term effects of inhaled pollutants upon the population, of which a percentage may be particularly susceptible because of the presence of certain diseases and conditions.

Nonetheless, there is firm evidence that cigarette smoking in various indoor environments – automobiles, buses, offices, homes, restaurants, etc. – may give rise to levels of specific pollutants well above those normally found in everyday situations in the absence of cigarette smoke and these levels often exceed standards for human exposure, where such standards exist. This finding has repeatedly been observed in actual and experimental conditions for the major constituents of cigarette smoke – carbon monoxide, nicotine and total particulates. The long-term effects of exposure in passive cigarette smoking situations to other identified smoke constituents, which occur in lower and trace amounts, are not known.

APPENDIX II

Excerpts from Judgment and Opinion – Shimp vs. New Jersey Bell

SUPERIOR COURT OF NEW JERSEY

CHANCERY DIVISION, SALEM COUNTY

Civil Action, Docket No. C-2904-75

DONNA M. SHIMP,

Plaintiff,

vs.

NEW JERSEY BELL TELEPHONE COMPANY,

Defendant.

JUDGMENT

IT IS ON THIS 25th day of March, 1977,
ORDERED AND ADJUDGED:

1. That defendant New Jersey Bell Telephone Company provide safe working conditions for plaintiff, by restricting the smoking of employees to the non-work area presently used as a lunch room.

2. That no smoking shall be permitted in the offices or adjacent customer service area of plaintiff's place of employment.

3. That defendant New Jersey Bell Telephone Company provide access to wash room facilities for the plaintiff through a separate entrance other than through the Manager's office.

4. That defendant New Jersey Bell Telephone Company inform any managerial employee that he or she is directed and that they must comply with the Orders of this Court.

5. That the Orders and Judgements rendered in this matter be enforced by the defendant New Jersey Bell Telephone Company without any harrassment of the plaintiff of any type or description, including but not limited to work assignments and duties, and conditions of employment.

HON. PHILIP A. GRUCCIO, J.S.C.

THE OPINION

Excerpts:

This case involves a matter of first impression in this State: whether a non smoking employee is denied a safe working environment and entitled to injunctive relief when forced by proximity to smoking employees to involuntarily inhale "second-hand" cigarette smoke.

Plaintiff seeks to have cigarette smoking enjoined in the area where she works. She alleges that her employer defendant N.J. Bell Telephone Co. is causing her to work in an unsafe environment by refusing to enact a ban against smoking in the office where she works. The company allows other employees to smoke while on the job at desks situated in the same work area as that of plaintiff. Plaintiff contends that the passive inhalation of smoke and the gaseous byproducts of burning tobacco is deleterious to her health. Therefore her employer by permitting employees to smoke in the work area is allowing an unsafe condition to exist. The present action is a suit to enjoin these allegedly unsafe conditions thereby restoring to plaintiff a healthy environment in which to work...

It is clearly the law in this State that an employee has a right to work in a safe environment. An employer is under an affirmative duty to provide a work area that is free from unsafe conditions. MacDonald v. Standard Oil, 69 N.J.L. 445 (E. & A. 1903); Burns v. Del. and Atl. Telegraph and Telephone Co., 70 N.J.L. 745 (E. & A. 1904); Clayton v. Ainsworth, 122 N.J.L. 160 (E. & A. 1939); Davis v. N.J. Zinc Co., 116 N.J.L. 103 (E. & A. 1936); Canonico v. Celanese Corp. of America, 11 N.J. Super. 445 (App. Div. 1951), certif. den. 7 N.J. 77 (1951)...

In Canonico v. Celanese Corp. of America, supra, plaintiff was seeking to recover damages for illness allegedly contracted from the inhalation of cellulose acetate dust. The dust was a result of the manufacturing process in which plaintiff was employed. His job location was in the pulverizing room where as much as 400 pounds of dust could be present and circulating in the air in a single day. The court reiterated the common law premise that it is the master's duty to use reasonable care to provide a proper and safe place for the servant to work and that failure to use reasonable diligence to protect the employee from unnecessary risks will cause the employer to be answerable for the damages which ensue. The court upheld the trial court's dismissal of the cause of action emphasizing that cellulose acetate dust is a non toxic result of the manufacturing process.

Two important distinctions are found between the Canonico decision and the case presently at bar. In Canonico the court was presented with a byproduct which was a **necessary result** of the operation of the business. There is no way to pulverize cellulose acetate material without creating dust. The denial of recovery for an occupational disease where the nature of the risk is obvious or known to the employee is based on the theory that the employee assumes the risk as ordinarily incident to his employment.

• • •

Canonico v. Celanese Corp. of America, supra; Zebrowski v. Warner Sugar Co., 83 N.J.L. 558 (E. & A. 1912). Plaintiff's complaint here arises from the presence of cigarette smoke in the atmosphere of her work environment. Cigarette smoke, unlike cellulose dust, is not a natural byproduct of N.J. Bell's business. Plaintiff works in an office. The tools of her trade are pens, pencils, paper, a typewriter and a telephone. There is no necessity to fill the air with tobacco smoke in order to carry on defendant's business, so it cannot be regarded as an occupational hazard which plaintiff has voluntarily assumed in pursuing a career as a secretary...

Where an employer is under a common law duty to act, a court of equity may enforce an employee's rights by ordering the employer to eliminate any preventable hazardous condition which the court finds to exist. The courts of New Jersey have long been open to protect basic employees' rights by injunction...

Since plaintiff has a common law right to a safe working environment, the issue remains whether the work area here is unsafe due to a preventable hazard which I may enjoin. There can be no doubt that the byproducts of burning tobacco are toxic and dangerous to the health of smokers and non smokers generally and this plaintiff in particular...

The evidence is clear and overwhelming. Cigarette smoke contaminates and pollutes the air, creating a health hazard not merely to the smoker but to all those around her who must rely upon the same air supply. The right of an individual to risk his or her own health does not include the right to jeopardize the health of those who must remain around him or her in order to properly perform the duties of their jobs. The portion of the population which is especially sensitive to cigarette smoke is so significant that it is reasonable to expect an employer to foresee health consequences and to impose upon him a duty to abate the hazard which causes the discomfort. I order New Jersey Bell Telephone Company to do so.

In determining the extent to which smoking must be restricted the rights and interests of smoking and non smoking employees alike must be considered. The employee's right to a safe working environment makes it clear that smoking must be forbidden in the work area. The employee who desires to smoke on his own time, during coffee breaks and lunch hours should have a reasonably accessible area in which to smoke. In the present case, the employees' lunchroom and lounge could serve this function. Such a rule imposes no hardship upon defendant New Jersey Bell Telephone Company. The company already has in effect a rule that cigarettes may not be smoked around the telephone equipment. The rationale behind the rule is that the machines are extremely sensitive and can be damaged by the smoke. Human beings are also very sensitive and can be damaged by cigarette smoke. Unlike a piece of machinery, the damage to a human is all too often irreparable. If a circuit or wiring goes bad, the company can install a replacement part. It is not so simple in the case of a human lung, eye or heart. The parts are hard to come by if indeed they can be found at all.

A company which has demonstrated such concern for its mechanical components should have at least as much concern for its human beings. Plaintiff asks nothing more than to be able to breathe the air in its clear and natural state [emphasis added].

Accordingly, I order defendant New Jersey Bell Telephone Company to provide safe working conditions for plaintiff by restricting the smoking of employees to the non work area presently used as a lunchroom. No smoking shall be permitted in the offices or adjacent customer service area.

It is so ordered.

APPENDIX III

Major Toxic and Tumorigenic Agents of Cigarette Smoke: Ratio of Sidestream Smoke (SS) to Mainstream Smoke (MS)

A Gas Phase	Mainstream Smoke/Cigarette			SS/MS
Carbon dioxide	10	- 80	mg	8.1
Carbon monoxide	0.5	- 26	mg	2.5
Nitrogen oxides (NO)	16	- 600	μg	4.7 - 5.8
Ammonia	10	- 130	μg	44 - 73
Hydrogen cyanide	280	- 550	μg	0.17 - 0.37
Hydrazine		32	μg	3
Formaldehyde	20	- 90	μg	51
Acetone	100	- 940	μg	2.5 - 3.2
Acrolein	10	- 140	μg	12
Acetonitrile	60	- 160	μg	10
Pyridine		32	μg	10
3-Vinylpyridine		23	μg	28
N-Nitrosodimethylamine	4	- 180	ng	10 - 830
N-Nitrosoethylmethylamine	1.0	- 40	ng	5 - 12
N-Nitrosodiethylamine	0.1	- 28	ng	4 - 25
N-Nitrosopyrrolidine	0	- 110	ng	3 - 76

B Particulate Phase	Mainstream Smoke/Cigarette			SS/MS		
Total particulate phase	0.1	-	40	mg	1.3 -	1.9
Nicotine	0.06	-	2.3	mg	2.6 -	3.3
Toluene			108	μg		5.6
Phenol	20	-	150	μg		2.6
Catechol	40	-	280	μg		0.7
Stigmasterol			53	μg		0.8
Total phytosterols			130	μg		0.8
Naphthalene			2.8	μg		16
1-Methylnaphthalene			1.2	μg		26
2-Methylnaphthalene			1.0	μg		29
Phenanthrene	2.0	-	80	ng		2.1
Benz(a)anthracine	10	-	70	ng		2.7
Pyrene	15	-	90	ng	1.9 -	3.6
Benzo(a)pyrene	8	-	40	ng	2.7 -	3.4
Quinoline			1.7	μg		11
Methylquinoline			6.7	μg		11
Harmane	1.1	-	3.1	μg	0.7 -	2.7
Norharmane	3.2	-	8.1	μg	1.4 -	4.3
Aniline	100	-	1200	ng		30
0-Toluidine			32	ng		19
1-Naphthylamine	1.0	-	22	ng		39
2-Naphthylamine	4.3	-	27	ng		39
4-Aminobiphenyl	2.4	-	4.6	ng		31
N-Nitrosonornicotine	0.2	-	3.7	μg	1 -	5
NNK*	0.12	-	0.44	μg	1 -	8
N-Nitrosoanatabine	0.15	-	4.6	μg	1 -	7
N-Nitrosodiethanolamine	0	-	40	μg		1.2
Polonium-210	0.03	-	0.5	pc		NA

*NNK = 4(Methylnitrosamino)-1-(3-pyridyl)-1-butanone

SOURCE: U.S. Department of Health and Human Services. *The Health Consequences of Smoking: Cancer – A Report of the Surgeon General.* Washington, U.S. Government Print Office, 1982.

NA = Not available.

APPENDIX IV

Known and Probable Human Carcinogens in Tobacco Smoke, as determined by the International Agency for Research on Cancer (IARC) and the American Conference of Governmental Industrial Hygienists (ACGIH)

SUBSTANCE	STATUS OF HUMAN CARCINOGEN		THRESHOLD LIMIT VALUE
	Known	Probable	Assigned by ACGIH
Acrylonitrile	ACGIH		4.5 mg/m³
Vinyl Chloride	IARC, ACGIH		10 mg/m³
2-naphthylamine	IARC, ACGIH		0
4-aminobiphenyl	IARC, ACGIH		0
Arsenic	IARC		0.2 mg/m³
Benzene	IARC	ACGIH	30 mg/m³
Soots, tars & oils	IARC		–
Whole tobacco smoke	IARC		–
Benzo(a)pyrene		IARC, ACGIH	no TLV assigned
Formaldehyde		IARC, ACGIH	1.5 mg/m³
Hydrazine		IARC, ACGIH	0.1 mg/m³
N-nitrosodimethylamine		ACGIH	no TLV assigned – avoidance of exposure recommended
Nickel		IARC	1.0 mg/m³
Cadmium		IARC	0.05 mg/m³

SOURCES: American Conference of Governmental Industrial Hygienists.
Documentation of the Threshold Limit Values – Fourth Edition, 1980 with Supplemental Documentation, 1981, 1982 and 1983. Cincinnati, ACGIH, 1980.
International Agency for Research on Cancer.
Chemicals, Industrial Processes and Industries Associated with Cancer in Humans. IARC Monographs, Volumes 1 to 29, Supplement 4. Lyon, IARC, 1982.

APPENDIX V

City of San Francisco

**Excerpts from Smoking Pollution Control Ordinance No. 298-83
Passed by the San Francisco Board of Supervisors May 31, 1983.**

Sec. 1001. Purpose. Because the smoking of tobacco or any other weed or plant is a danger to health and is a cause of material annoyance and discomfort to those who are present in confined places, the Board of Supervisors hereby declares that the purpose of this article is to protect the public health and welfare by prohibiting smoking in the office workplace. This ordinance is intended to minimize the toxic effects of smoking in the office workplace by requiring an employer to adopt a policy that will accommodate, insofar as possible, the preferences of nonsmokers and smokers.

Sec. 1003. (b) If an accommodation which is satisfactory to all affected nonsmoking employees cannot be reached in any given office workplace, the preferences of nonsmoking employees shall prevail and the employer shall prohibit smoking in that office workplace. Where the employer prohibits smoking in an office workplace, the area in which smoking is prohibited shall be clearly marked with signs.

Sec. 1005. Penalties and Enforcement.

(1) The Director of Public Health shall enforce Section 1003 hereof against violations by either of the following actions.
   (a) Serving notice requiring the correction of any violation of this Article;
   (b) Calling upon the City Attorney to maintain an action for injunction to enforce the provisions of this Article, to cause the correction of any such violation, and for assessment and recovery of a civil penalty for such violation;
(2) Any employer who violates Section 1003 hereof may be liable for a civil penalty, not to exceed $500, which penalty shall be assessed and recovered in a civil action brought in the name of the People of the City and County of San Francisco in any court of competent jurisdiction. Each day such violation is committed or permitted to continue shall constitute a separate offense and shall be punishable as such. Any penalty assessed and recovered in an action brought pursuant to this paragraph shall be paid to the Treasurer of the City and County of San Francisco.

APPENDIX VI

Sample Letter to Management by the Physician of a Nonsmoking Employee

I am the family physician of George W., who is employed by your company in the shipping department.

Mr. W., who is a nonsmoker, experiences the following symptoms as a result of exposure to second-hand tobacco smoke in his work area: headaches, drowsiness, burning and tearing eyes and a dry cough. These responses make it difficult for Mr. W. to do his job or to receive the normal satisfaction which is associated with being a productive, conscientious employee.

He is also concerned, with justification, about the adverse effects associated with long-term exposure to the toxic particulates and gases in second-hand tobacco smoke. It is now well-established that second-hand tobacco smoke is not simply a nuisance. Such smoke contains more than 50 substances capable of causing cancer and numerous studies have confirmed that prolonged exposure may represent a serious health risk to non-smokers. This can include significant lung impairment and increased risk of illness and early death.

It is my professional opinion that smoking in the workplace is incompatible with good health, particularly in view of the prolonged exposure times involved for nonsmokers. Given that my patient is able to perform job assignments in a satisfactory manner except for the presence of tobacco smoke which exacerbates his medical condition, I fully endorse Mr. W.'s request for measures that will remove this hazard from his working environment.

[If you are suffering from a pre-existing health condition that forces you to remain away from work until action is taken, your doctor may wish to substitute the following for the previous paragraph:

It is my professional opinion that smoking in the workplace is incompatible with good health, particularly in view of the prolonged exposure times involved for nonsmokers. Furthermore, my patient is able to perform job assignments in a satisfactory manner except for the presence of tobacco smoke which exacerbates his medical condition. Until such time as an effective remedy is provided, I have advised my patient to remain away from work until air quality in his workplace improves.]

I would be grateful for an early reply with respect to your views on this matter.

Signed,

_____, M.D.

Note: We recommend that your physician append to his/her letter the most up-to-date medical article available. At the time of publication we recommend N. E. Collishaw, J. Kirkbride, D. T. Wigle, "Tobacco smoke in the workplace: An occupational health hazard," **The Canadian Medical Association Journal,** Vol. 131, November 15, 1984.

APPENDIX VII

Sample Grievance

I (We) grieve Management's refusal to provide me (us) with a safe and healthy work environment by refusing either (a) to prohibit smoking on company premises or (b) to restrict smoking to enclosed, separately ventilated areas for smokers.

Second-hand tobacco smoke (exhaled tobacco smoke combined with smoke from idling cigarettes, cigars and pipes) contains carcinogens and other toxic compounds. Second-hand tobacco smoke is a discomfort, can impair breathing and is a serious health hazard to non-smokers.

I (We) submit that Management's refusal in this instance is a violation of Article XXX of the Collective Agreement which states that "the Employer Shall...make all reasonable provisions for the occupational safety and health of employees."

Management already prohibits smoking in certain work locations, such as the EDP area and fiche laboratory, on the grounds that tobacco smoke is detrimental to the functioning of the equipment. It is not unreasonable to provide the same degree of protection of human health that is presently provided to protect the health of the mechanical equipment in my (our) workplace.

Redress Desired

That my (our) concerns for health be respected and that smoking be prohibited on company premises or restricted to enclosed, separately ventilated smoking areas,

that such remedies be implemented without delay, and

that this smoke-free work environment be provided without adversely affecting my (our) conditions of employment or rate of pay.

APPENDIX VIII

Sample Application to Medical Officer of Health

In the following sample letter, a nonsmoker employed by an Ontario company lodges a complaint about second-hand smoke in the workplace under the Ontario Health Protection and Promotion Act (1984).

Dr._____
Medical Officer of Health
Your municipality or region

Dear Dr._____

I am an employee of _____ Corporation, 123 Main Road, Hamilton, where I work as a word processing operator. As a nonsmoker, I am having a severe problem with second-hand tobacco smoke in my workplace.

There are 10 people working in my section, and three are smokers who smoke at regular intervals throughout the day. By the end of the day my eyes are usually smarting and I frequently get headaches from the smoke. Sometimes I have to leave my work area for a breath of fresh air. (If you have more severe reactions or have visited your physician about the problem, make this clear here.)

On several occasions I have asked the smokers to refrain from smoking in the general work area but they have refused. I asked my supervisor to do something about the problem but she also refused on the grounds that a restriction on smoking would violate the rights of smokers.

I am extremely worried about the long-term effects of this situation on my health. Since I have been unable to obtain relief through my own efforts, I am hereby requesting your intervention and assistance under Sec. 11 of the Ontario Health Protection and Promotion Act (1984).

In support of this request I have attached a bulletin from Health and Welfare Canada, **Chronic Diseases in Canada,** Vol. 3 (1) June 1982 [available from the Non-Smokers' Rights Association office] which shows that second-hand tobacco smoke contains many known and probable carcinogens. Two of these, 2-Naphthylamine and 4-Aminobiphenyl, have been assigned a Threshold Level Value of Zero by the American Conference of Governmental and Industrial Hygienists (ACGIH), meaning that no exposure of any kind is to be permitted. A third substance, N-Nitrosodimethylamine (NDMA), has produced cancer in all animal species on which it has been tested[1]

Please allow me to quote from a 1984 Health and Welfare Canada report entitled "Tobacco smoke in the workplace: An occupational health hazard":

> "Tobacco smoke, which contains over 50 known carcinogens and many other toxic agents, is a health hazard for nonsmokers who are regularly exposed to it while at work. Involuntary exposure to tobacco smoke annoys and irritates many healthy nonsmokers. Serious acute health effects are probably limited to the one fifth of the population with pre-existing health conditions that are aggravated by exposure to tobacco smoke. The consequences of long-term exposure include decreased lung function and lung cancer. Existing air quality standards for workplaces do not directly address the question of an acceptable level for tobacco smoke. The evidence on the composition of tobacco smoke and on the health hazards of involuntary exposure suggests that there may not be a 'safe level' for such exposure."[2]

In view of the above, I respectfully submit that second-hand smoke in my workplace is a health hazard as defined in Sec. 1, Para. 9 of the **Ontario Health Protection and Promotion Act,** namely:

> "A condition of premises, a substance, thing, plant or animal other than man, or a solid, liquid, gas or combination of any of them, that has or that is likely to have an adverse effect on the health of any person."

May I ask further that the investigation of my complaint include an air test in my workplace which is designed for the specific purpose of measuring the contaminants in tobacco smoke, and particularly those occurring in the particulate phase?

Yours sincerely,

---

1. **Chronic Diseases in Canada,** Vol. 3 (1) June, 1982, p. 5

2. By: Neil Collishaw, Chief, Policy Analysis, Bureau of Tobacco Control, Health Protection Branch: John Kirkbride, Director, Occupational Health Unit, Medical Services Branch; Donald Wigle, Chief, Non-Communicable Diseases Division, Bureau of Epidemiology, Health Protection Branch, **The Canadian Medical Association Journal,** Vol. 131, November 15, 1984, pp. 1199-1204.

APPENDIX IX

Excerpts from Ajudication Hearing

BEFORE THE PUBLIC SERVICE STAFF RELATIONS BOARD UNDER THE PUBLIC SERVICE STAFF RELATIONS ACT

BETWEEN:

PETER WILSON,

Grievor,

AND:

TREASURY BOARD (Health & Welfare Canada),

Employer.

BEFORE: Walter L. Nisbet, Q.C., Deputy Chairman.

Heard in Ottawa, February 20, 21, 22, March 6 and 7 and May 16; and in Toronto on March 14 and 15, 1985.

REASONS FOR DECISION

126. The provisions of the Dangerous Substances Safety Standard relevant to this grievance are as follows:

5. In this Standard:
   (1) "dangerous substance" means any substance, that because of a property it possesses is dangerous to the safety or health of any person who is exposed to it;

• • •

12. Any dangerous substance that may be carried by the air is to be confined as closely as is reasonably practicable to its source.

13. Subject to paragraph 14, each department shall ensure that the concentration of any dangerous substance that may be carried by the air in any area where an employee is working:

   (1) does not exceed the threshold limit value recommended by the American Conference of Governmental Industrial Hygienists in its pamphlet 'Threshold Limit Values for

Airborne Contaminants 1976', as amended from time to time; or

(2) conforms with any standard that follows good industrial safety practices, and is recommended by Labour Canada or Health and Welfare Canada.

14. Except in respect of any dangerous substance that is assigned a Ceiling 'C' value by the American Conference of Governmental Industrial Hygienists, it is permissible for the concentration of a dangerous substance that may be carried by the air in the area where an employee is working to exceed the threshold limit value described in paragraph 13 for a period of time calculated according to a formula that:

(i) is prescribed by the American Conference of Governmental Industrial Hygienists; or

(ii) is recommended by Labour Canada or Health and Welfare Canada.

15. Where the atmosphere of any area in which an employee is working is subject to contamination by a dangerous substance, the atmosphere is to be sampled and tested by a qualified person as frequently

(1) as may be necessary to ensure that the level of contamination does not at any time exceed the safe limits prescribed by paragraphs 13 and 14; or

(2) as may be recommended by Labour Canada or Health and Welfare Canada.

16. The sampling and testing referred to in paragraph 15 shall comply with

(1) a method recommended by the American Conference of Governmental Industrial Hygienists, the American Society for testing and materials, the Dominion Fire Commissioner; or

(2) any other sampling and testing method that follows good industrial safety practice, and is recommended by Labour Canada, Health and Welfare Canada or the Dominion Fire Commissioner.

• • •

20. Each employee whose safety or health may be endangered by exposure to a dangerous substance or radiation emitting device is to be informed of the danger.

• • •

27. Where there are a number of substances in the air in different areas of a workplace, a combination of which might cause a hazard, the air is to be exhausted from those areas in such a

manner that the various substances are not combined.

28. Exhaust and inlet ducts for ventilation systems are to be located and arranged so as to ensure that air contaminated with dangerous substances does not enter areas occupied by employees.

29. Departments shall ensure that:

    (1) premises and equipment are, to the extent that is reasonably practicable, designed, constructed and maintained in a manner that will

        (a) prevent the dust and waste from dangerous substances from accumulating in dangerous quantities, and;

        (b) facilitate the easy removal of the dust and waste referred to in paragraph 29 (1) (a);

    (2) all dust, waste material and any spill of a dangerous substance is

        (a) removed from its premises in such a manner and as frequently as will ensure a safe and healthful environment for employees, and

        (b) disposed of in a manner that does not endanger the health and safety of any employee.

• • •

34. Measures and precautions concerning smoking, or any procedure or equipment the use of which in a restricted area may cause ignition or explosion of a dangerous substance, shall be in compliance with the requirements of the Dominion Fire Commissioner.

• • •

49. Where recommended by Health and Welfare Canada, appropriate records are to be maintained in respect to an employee's exposure to dangerous substances which may have an accumulative effect on the health of the employee.

• • •

137. I have conducted a careful analysis and review of all of the expert testimony and I have come to the conclusion that, on a balance of probabilities, the evidence presented on behalf of the grievor establishes the existence of a statistically significant co-relation between exposure to passive smoke and an increased incidence of lung cancer. As a consequence, I find that passive tobacco smoke is a "dangerous substance" within the meaning of the Standard.

138. Passive tobacco smoke may be carried by the air and is therefore to be confined as closely as is reasonably practicable to its source, pursuant to section 12 of the Standard. The employer was in a breach of this provision as it made no attempt to confine the passive tobacco smoke present in the grievor's workplace as closely as was reasonably practicable to its source. The only practical means by which the employer may meet this obligation is to provide separately ventilated areas for smokers who are required to work in the same area as the grievor.

139. The areas in which the grievor worked were subject to contamination by passive tobacco smoke. As a consequence, the employer pursuant to section 15 of the Standard had an obligation to sample and test the atmosphere in the workplace as frequently as might be necessary to ensure that the level of contamination did not at any time exceed the safe limits prescribed by sections 13 and 14, or as may be recommended by Labour Canada or Health and Welfare Canada. The evidence is that the employer conducted only superficial tests of the air quality in the grievor's workplace and, in particular, failed to test for 4-aminobiphenyl and beta-naphthylamine to which exposure is not to be permitted "—by any route—respiratory, skin, or oral, as detected by the most sensitive methods—", according to the threshold limit values published by the American Conference of Governmental Industrial Hygienists which are incorporated by reference into the Standard (Exhibit G-4, page 41). For these reasons I find that the employer was in breach of section 15 of the Standard.

140. As the grievor no longer occupies the same workplace as he did when he filed his grievance, I am not prepared to make a mandatory order directed to the employer in this case. The evidence is that the employer made some effort to comply with the collective agreement by conducting the sampling and testing described in Exhibit E-24.

141. Accordingly, I declare that, on the date the grievance was filed, the employer was in breach of the Dangerous Substances Safety Standard which forms part of the relevant collective agreement in that it failed:

   (a) to confine tobacco smoke at the grievor's workplace as closely as was reasonably practicable to its source;

   (b) to sample and test the atmosphere at the grievor's workplace as frequently as necessary to ensure that the level of contamination by tobacco smoke and its constituents did not at any time exceed the safe limits prescribed by sections 13 and 14 of the Standard;

   (c) to sample and test the atmosphere at the grievor's workplace for the purpose of determining the presence of beta-naphthylamine and 4-aminobiphenyl for which no threshold limit values are given in Exhibit 4; and

(d) to provide separately ventilated areas for smokers working in the same workplace as the grievor to ensure that the tobacco smoke they produce is confined as closely as was reasonably practicable to its source.

142. To that extent, the grievance is upheld.

Walter L. Nisbet, Q.C.,
Deputy Chairman.

OTTAWA, December 20, 1985

Notes

1 From an advertisement in the NEW YORK STATE JOURNAL OF MEDICINE, December 1983, p. 1344.

2 N. Collishaw, "Deaths Attributable to Smoking – Canada, 1979," CHRONIC DISEASES IN CANADA, Health and Welfare Canada, 3 (1) June 1982 p. 3.

3 Morley Swingle, "The Legal Conflict Between Smokers and Nonsmokers: The Majestic Vice Versus the Right to Clean Air," MISSOURI LAW REVIEW, 45 (51) (1980) p. 449.

4 C. B. Barad, "Smoking on the Job: The Controversy Heats Up," OCCUPATIONAL HEALTH AND SAFETY, 48 (1979) p. 21.

5 Roy Shephard and Robert Labarre, "Attitudes of the Public Towards Cigarette Smoke in Public Places," CANADIAN JOURNAL OF PUBLIC HEALTH, 69, JULY-AUGUST 1978, p. 307.

6 James Repace and Alfred Lowrey, "Indoor Air Pollution," ENVIRONMENT INTERNATIONAL, 8 (1982) p. 21.

7 T. Hirayama, "Nonsmoking Wives of Heavy Smokers Have a Higher Risk of Lung Cancer: A Study from Japan," 282 (1981) pp. 183-5.

8 D. Trichopoulos, A. Kalandidi, L. Sparros and B. MacMahon, "Lung Cancer and Passive Smoking," INTERNATIONAL JOURNAL OF CANCER, 27 (1981).

9 P. Correa, L. W. Pickle, E. Fontham et al., "Passive Smoking and Lung Cancer," LANCET, 2, Sep. 10, 1983, pp. 595-7.

10 D. P. Sandler, R. B. Everson and A. J. Wilcox, "Passive Smoking in Adulthood and Cancer Risk," AMERICAN JOURNAL OF EPIDEMIOLOGY, 121 (1) 1985, p. 37.

11 James Repace and Alfred Lowrey, "A Quantitative Estimate of Nonsmokers' Lung Cancer Risk from Passive Smoking," in press, ENVIRONMENT INTERNATIONAL.

12 J. R. White and H. F. Froeb, "Small Airways Dysfunction in Nonsmokers Chronically Exposed to Tobacco Smoke," NEW ENGLAND JOURNAL OF MEDICINE, 302 (1980).

13 F. Kauffmann, J-F. Tessier and P. Oriol, "Adult Passive Smoking in the Home Environment: A Risk Factor for Chronic Airflow Limitation," AMERICAN JOURNAL OF EPIDEMIOLOGY, 117 (1983) pp. 269-80.

14 U.S. Department of Health, Education and Welfare, "SMOKING AND HEALTH: A REPORT OF THE SURGEON GENERAL," Washington: U.S. Government Printing Office, 1979 (DHEW Publication No. [PHS] 79-50066).

Also: R. Steele and J. T. Langworth, "The Relationship of Antenatal and Postnatal Factors to Sudden Unexpected Death in Infancy," CANADIAN MEDICAL ASSOCIATION JOURNAL, 94 (1966) pp. 1165-71.

Also: A. B. Bergman and L. A. Wiesner, "Relationship of Passive Cigarette Smoking to Sudden Infant Death Syndrome," PEDIATRICS, 58 (1976) pp. 665-8.

15 Peter Fong, "The Hazard of Cigarette Smoking to Nonsmokers," JOURNAL OF BIOLOGICAL PHYSICS, 10 (1982).

16 Canada Health Survey, special tabulation covering 1978-9 (1982).

17 "THE HEALTH CONSEQUENCES OF SMOKING, A REPORT OF THE [U.S.] SURGEON GENERAL", 1972, U.S. Department of Health, Education and Welfare, Public Health Service, pp. 1967.

18 R. J. C. Harris and G. Negroni, "Production of Lung Carcinomas in C 57 BL Mice Exposed to a Cigarette Smoke and Air Mixture," BRITISH MEDICAL JOURNAL (4) Dec. 16, 1967, pp. 637-41.

19 MORNINGSIDE program, CBC Radio, Nov. 16, 1978.
20 D. T. Wigle, "Tobacco Smoke and the Nonsmoker", CHRONIC DISEASES, op. cit., p. 5.
21 Copyright 1984 by R. J. Reynolds Tobacco Co.
22 Published by The Bodley Head (Toronto 1984) p. 44.
23 Staff Report on the Cigarette Advertising Investigation, May 1981, pp. 2-13.
24 Ibid.
25 NEW YORK STATE JOURNAL OF MEDICINE, 83 (13) December 1983, p. 1280.
26 Cited in the (Isabelle) REPORT OF THE STANDING COMMITTEE ON HEALTH, WELFARE AND SOCIAL AFFAIRS ON TOBACCO AND CIGARETTE SMOKING, Ottawa: Queen's Printer (1969) p. 10.
27 Royal College of Physicians, SMOKING AHD HEALTH NOW, London, (Pitman) 1971.
28 "THE HEALTH CONSEQUENCES OF SMOKING" (1983) p. 7.
29 "THE HEALTH CONSEQUENCES OF SMOKING" (1982) pp. v-vi.
30 "Before You Hire Smokers", presented at the annual meeting of FANS (Fresh Air for Nonsmokers) Seattle, Wash., June 22, 1981, p. 10.
31 Speaking at the First World Conference on Smoking and Health, New York City, 1967.
32 "Time for Action on Passive Smoking", CANADIAN MEDICAL ASSOCIATION JOURNAL, 127, Nov. 1, 1982, p. 810.
33 B. Rogers and L. Mulligan, "World-Wide Cigarette Consumption, 1983", CHRONIC DISEASES IN CANADA, 5, March 1985.
34 N. Collishaw and L. Mulligan, "Recent Trends in Tobacco Consumption in Canada and Other Countries", CHRONIC DISEASES, 4 (1984) pp. 52-4.

Canada's daily cigarette consumption rate is calculated by N. Collishaw, Chief of Policy Analysis, Bureau of Tobacco Control, Health Protection Branch, Health and Welfare Canada, based on the following figures for 1984:

Sales of manufactured cigarettes (Statistics Canada Cat. No. 32-022)	61.7 billion
Sales of fine cut tobacco (Cat. No. 32-022)	6.16 million K
[At 1 gram per cigarette, equivalent to 6.16 billion cigarettes]	
Total manufactured cigarettes and equivalents	67.9 billion
Canadian population 18 years and older (Statistics Canada)	18.5 million
Number of adult smokers (39% of total)	7.2 million
Average daily per capita consumption	26 cigarettes

35 The percentage of Canadian smokers is based on a Canada Labor Survey conducted in December 1983 which showed 32 per cent of Canadians 20 years of age and older as smokers. Since these surveys rely on proxy reporting, Health and Welfare Canada researchers suggest that the result should be corrected upward by 3-4 per cent. They also suggest that Gallup poll results based on the question "Have you, yourself, smoked any cigarettes in the past week?" be adjusted downward 2.5 to 3% to remove occasional smokers. [Based on a Feb. 25, 1985 telephone conversation with Wayne Millar, Health Promotion Studies Unit, Health Promotion Directorate, Health and Welfare Canada.]

The percentage of U.S. smokers in 1983 is provided by the U.S. Division of Health Interview Statistics, Atlantic, Ga., which does not rely on proxy reporting.

36 Author's calculation based on Statistics Canada sales figures for 1983.

37 James Repace and Alfred Lowrey, "Modelling Exposure of Nonsmokers to Ambient Tobacco Smoke," report presented to the annual meeting of the Air Pollution Control Association, Atlanta, Ga., June 19-24, 1983, p. 2.

38 Ibid., p. 1.

39 Ibid., abstract.

40 M. A. H. Russell and C. Feyerabend, "Blood and Urinary Nicotine in Nonsmokers," LANCET, 1 (1973) pp. 576-9.

41 S. Matsukura, T. Taminato et al., "Effects of Environmental Tobacco Smoke on Urinary Cotinine Excretion in Nonsmokers: Evidence for Passive Smoking," THE NEW ENGLAND JOURNAL OF MEDICINE, 311 (13) Sept. 27, 1984, p. 828.

42 Donna Shimp, Alfred Blumrosen and Stuart Finifter, HOW TO PROTECT YOUR HEALTH AT WORK (Published by Environmental Improvement Associates, Salem, N.J.) p. 117.

43 R. P. Bos, J. L. G. Theuws and P. T. Henderson, "Excretion of Mutagens in Human Urine after Passive Smoking," CANCER LETTERS, 19, 1982, pp. 85-90.

44 "Tobacco Smoke: The Double Standard," a report from the Centre for Philosophy and Public Policy (University of Maryland) 4 (1) Winter (1984) p. 6.

45 "Modelling Exposure of Nonsmokers," op. cit., abstract.

46 White and Froeb, "Small Airways Dysfunction," op. cit.

47 U.S. Department of Health and Human Services, "THE HEALTH CONSEQUENCES OF SMOKING: CANCER: A REPORT OF THE SURGEON GENERAL" (DHHS [PHS] 82-50179) Rockville, Md., 1982.
Also: U.S. Department of Health, Education and Welfare, "SMOKING AND HEALTH: A REPORT OF THE SURGEON GENERAL" (DHEW Pub. No. [PHS] 79-50066) Rockville, Md., 1979.
Also: International Agency for Research on Cancer, "Chemicals, Industrial Processes and Industries Associated with Cancer in Humans," IARC Monographs 1-29 Supp. 4, Lyon, 1982, pp. 14-16.
Other researchers have estimated the number of carcinogens in the particulate phase of tobacco smoke to be as high as 60 (see Note 61).

48 International Agency for Research on Cancer, "Some N-Nitroso Compounds," IARC Monographs, 17, Lyon, 1978, pp. 125-75.

49 "The Health Consequences of Smoking: Cancer," see Note 47.

50 American Conference of Governmental Industrial Hygienists, "Threshold Limit Values for Chemical Substances and Physical Agents in the Workroom Environment," Cincinnatti: ACGIH Publications Office, 1981.

51 J. Tinker, "Should Smoking Be Banned?" NEW SCIENTIST, 59 (1973) p. 313.

52 D. T. Wigle, op. cit., p. 6.

53 Martin Dewey, "There's a Certain Air About Office Workers," THE GLOBE AND MAIL REPORT ON BUSINESS" [Toronto] May 24, 1980.

54 Ibid.

55 Ibid.

56 James Repace and Alfred Lowrey, "Tobacco Smoke, Ventilation and Indoor Air Quality," Paper: HO-82-6 (2) p. 903.

57 J. Repace, D. Seba, A. Lowrey and T. Gregory, "Effect of Negative Ion Generators on Ambient Tobacco Smoke," CLINICAL ECOLOGY 2 (2) Winter 1983/84, pp. 91-2.

58 "Tobacco Smoke, Ventilation and Indoor Air Quality," op. cit., p. 902.

59 "Effect of Ventilation on Passive Smoking Risk in a Model Workplace," abstract, proceedings of the Engineering Foundation Conference on Management of Atmospheres in Tightly Enclosed Spaces, Santa Barbara, Cal., Oct. 17-21, 1983.

60 "A Proposed Indoor Air Quality Standard for Ambient Tobacco Smoke," proceedings of the Conference on Indoor Air Quality and Climate, Stockholm, August, 1984, p. 3.

61 Telephone conversation with Repace, Oct. 31, 1984. Higher figures for carcinogenic substances in tobacco smoke appear to reflect new research. See Note 47.

62 James Repace, "Risks of Passive Smoking," working paper, Centre for Philosophy and Public Policy, p. 23.

63 W. Aronow, "Effects of Passive Smoking on Angina Pectoris," NEW ENGLAND JOURNAL OF MEDICINE, 229 (1978).

64 "Tobacco Smoke in the Workplace: An Occupational Health Hazard," CANADIAN MEDICAL ASSOCIATION JOURNAL, 131, Nov. 15, 1984, p. 1202.

65 See Note 50.

66 Quoted in IMPROVING THE WORK ENVIRONMENT, 2nd ed., published by Environmental Improvement Associates, Salem, N.J., 1984, p. 36.

67 See Note 60.

68 "Effect of Negative Ion Generators on Ambient Tobacco Smoke," op. cit., pp. 91 and 94.

69 Telephone conversation, March 7, 1985.

70 W. S. Rickert, J. C. Robinson and N. E. Collishaw, "Yields of Tar, Nicotine and Carbon Monoxide in the Sidestream Smoke from Fifteen Brands of Canadian Cigarettes," AMERICAN JOURNAL OF PUBLIC HEALTH, 74, March 1984, p. 229.

71 R. V. Ebert, M. E. McNabb, K. T. McCusker and S. L. Snow, "Amount of Nicotine and Carbon Monoxide Inhaled by Smokers of Low-Tar, Low-Nicotine Cigarettes," JOURNAL OF THE AMERICAN MEDICAL ASSOCIATION, 250 (20) Nov. 25, 1983, pp. 2840-2.
   Also: M. A. H. Russell, BANBURY REPORTS, 3, Cold Spring Harbor Laboratory, New York.
   Also: S. Schachter, "Nicotine Regulation in Heavy and Light Smokers," JOURNAL OF EXPERIMENTAL PSYCHOLOGY: GENERAL, 106 (1) 1977 pp. 5-12.

72 "Sickness Absence and Smoking Behavior and its Consequences," JOURNAL OF OCCUPATIONAL MEDICINE, 17 (7) July 1975, p. 444.

73 Neil Collishaw and Gordon Myers, "Dollar Estimates of the Consequences of Tobacco Use in Canada, 1979," CANADIAN JOURNAL OF PUBLIC HEALTH, 75, May-June, 1984 pp. 192-9.

74 S. Glantz and S. Schweitzer, "Savings and Costs Associated with the Clean Indoor Air Act of 1978," brief presented to the Office of the Legislative Analyst, State of California, August 1978, p. 3.

75 "How Much Can Business Expect to Earn from Smoking Cessation?" Paper presented at the National Interagency Council on Smoking and Health national conference: Smoking in the Workplace, Chicago, Ill., Jan. 9, 1980, p. 1.

76 See Note 30, pp. 3-7.

77 Quoted by Anne Kiefhaber and Willes Goldbeck in SMOKING: A CHALLENGE TO WORKSITE HEALTH MANAGEMENT.

78 Dow Chemical Company internal report and letter from William Fishbeck, M.D., Corporate Medical Dept., March 2, 1979.

79 David Smith, "Absenteeism and 'Presenteeism' in Industry," ARCHIVES OF ENVIRONMENTAL HEALTH, 21, November 1970, p. 674.

80 "Fire Department Hires Nonsmokers Only," CHRISTIAN SCIENCE MONITOR, Jan. 4, 1978, p. 6.

81 William Weis and Patrick Fleenor, "Cold-Shouldering the Smoker," September 1981, p. 31.

82 "Office Smokers Feel the Heat," Nov. 29, 1982, p. 102.

83 "Many Burned-Up Bosses Snuff Out the Employment Prospects of Smokers," April 15, 1982, p. 1.

84 DALLAS MORNING NEWS, reprinted in THE RED DEER ADVOCATE, November 1982.

85 Regina Carlson, "Now Companies Are Quitting Smoking Too," unpublished article, p. 12.

86 Telephone conversation with Mr. Carr, Corporate Director for Public Relations, September 1984.

87 Telephone conversation with Ian Smith, Director of Information, October 1984.

88 "Policies at Pratt and Whitney Aircraft," NONSMOKERS AND SMOKERS (Published by the American Lung Association), March 1982, p. 2.

89 Telephone conversation, September 1984.

90 "Many Burned-Up Bosses," op. cit.

91 Telephone conversation with Q. B. Welch, M.D., Chief, Office of Health Research Analysis, Kansas Department of Health and Environment, March 6, 1985.

92 Sept. 23, 1975.

93 Telephone conversation, October 1984.

94 Letter from Thomas Hill, Aetna vice president, to Ed Simone, Unigard Insurance Group, Bellevue, Wash.

95 Statement released at a press conference in Ottawa, Dec. 19, 1969. As chairman of the Canadian Tobacco Industries Ad Hoc Committee on Smoking and Health, Mr. Pare was commenting on the REPORT OF THE COMMONS STANDING COMMITTEE ON HEALTH, WELFARE AND SOCIAL AFFAIRS ON TOBACCO AND CIGARETTE SMOKING, known as the Isabelle report. See also note 26.

96 "A Word to Nonsmokers," THE NEW YORK TIMES MAGAZINE, Feb. 11, 1979, p. 83. The same advertisement appeared widely at this time.

97 "Time for Action on Passive Smoking," Nov. 1, 1982.

98 "Risks of Passive Smoking," op. cit., p. 23.

99 Letter, Nov. 30, 1977.

100 NEW YORK STATE JOURNAL OF MEDICINE, 83 (13) December 1983, p. 1248.

101 W. Pollin and R. T. Ravenholt, "Tobacco Addiction and Tobacco Mortality: Implications for Death Certification," JOURNAL OF THE AMERICAN MEDICAL ASSOCIATION, Special edition, 252 (20) Nov. 23-30, 1984, p. 2850.
Also: W. A. Hunt and D. A. Bespalec, "An Evaluation of Current Methods of Modifying Smoking Behavior," JOURNAL OF CLINICAL PSYCHOLOGY, 30 (4) pp. 431-8. The authors conclude that the average participant in the average smoking cessation program has a 15 to 20 per cent chance of being

abstinent six months or one year after the conclusion of the program.

Success rates for those enrolled in treatment programs for alcoholism appear to average between 26 and 32 per cent. [THE ADDICTIVE BEHAVIORS, ed. William R. Miller, Pergamon Press (1980) p. 13.]

It should be borne in mind that many smokers appear to quit without organized help, which suggests that over-all success rates for smoking cessation are higher than those produced by treatment programs. One British researcher estimates that 25 per cent of all smokers succeed in stopping permanently before age 60. [N. Lee, "Statistics of Smoking in the United Kingdom," Research Paper 1, London Tobacco Research Council, 1976.] Over-all success rates may be even higher than that, but the point remains: When an addiction has reached the point of requiring a program of therapy, success rates tend to be higher for alcoholics than for smokers.

102　In a follow-up of heroin addicts involved in a treatment program, it was found that 38.3 per cent of enrollees were either heroin-free or still successfully participating in the program four years after enrolling. [R. Smart, R. Segal, B. Ballah, A. Everson and J. Finley, "A Four-Year Follow-Up Study of Narcotic-Dependent Persons Receiving Methadone Maintenance Substitution Therapy," CANADIAN JOURNAL OF PUBLIC HEALTH, 68, Jan.-Feb. 1977.]

103　Gallup survey commissioned by the Health Promotion Directorate, Health and Welfare Canada, conducted in February 1984.

104　Figure for 1980, "Statistics on Alcohol and Drug Abuse in Canada and Other Countries," published by the Addiction Research Foundation, Toronto, 1982, Table 82: "Selected characteristics of the illicit narcotic drug users population in Canada, 1975-80."

105　Health and Welfare Canada, "Alcohol in Canada: A National Perspective," figure for 1980, p. 42.

106　Derived from N. E. Collishaw, John Kirkbride and D. T. Wigle, see Note 64.

107　See Note 73, pp. 192-9.

108　"Statistics on Alcohol and Drug Abuse in Canada and Other Countries," op. cit., data available by 1982.

109　See Note 2.

110　REPORT OF THE STANDING COMMITTEE ON HEALTH, WELFARE AND SOCIAL AFFAIRS ON TOBACCO AND CIGARETTE SMOKING, House of Commons Session 1969-70, p. 29.

111　Quoted by Count Egon Conti, A HISTORY OF SMOKING, London (1931).

112　"THE STRUCTURES OF EVERDAY LIFE: CIVILIZATION AND CAPITALISM 15TH - 18TH CENTURY," 1, New York: Harper, Row (1981) pp. 262-3.

113　London: Max Reinhardt (1976) p. 14.

114　"THE STRUCTURES OF EVERYDAY LIFE," op. cit., p. 264.

115　"Cigarette," ENCYCLOPEDIA BRITANNICA, 5 (1971) p. 768.

116　THE SMOKE RING. See Note 22. U.S. consumption p. 188, British consumption p. 41.

117　"Is Smoking on the Way Out?" CANADIAN BUSINESS MAGAZINE, December 1976, p. 48.

118　Statistics Canada, "Production and Distribution of Tobacco Products," Cat. No. 32-022.

119　"Now Companies Are Quitting Smoking Too," op. cit., p. 16.

120　"The Legal Conflict Between Smokers and Nonsmokers," p. 446.

121　Ibid., p. 450.

122　Ibid., p. 454.

123 San Francisco Municipal Code (Health Code), Art. 19, Sec. 1001.
124 Pasadena City Ordinance 6065.
125 Los Angeles City Ordinance 159498, passed Dec. 15, 1984.
126 "Attitudes of the Public," op. cit., p. 309.
127 Telephone conversation with MINNEAPOLIS TRIBUNE news staff, Sept. 1984.
128 Telephone conversation, May 17, 1984.
129 Personal conversation, Dec. 20, 1984.
130 January 1984, p. 5.
131 "Smoking at the Workplace: Legal Issues," NONSMOKERS AND SMOKERS, July 1983, p. 4.
132 SHIMP vs. NEW JERSEY BELL TELEPHONE CO., 368 A.2d 408.
133 "The Legal Conflict," op. cit., p. 466.
134 SMITH vs. WESTERN ELECTRIC CO., 1982 OSHD Para. 26, 256.
135 "Nonsmokers' Rights: Protection Against Involuntary Smoking in the Workplace," SUFFOLK UNIVERSITY LAW SCHOOL JOURNAL, 13 (2) Spring (1982) p. 28.
136 "The Legal Conflict," op. cit., p. 475.
137 January 1984, p. 4.
138 Ibid.
139 NONSMOKERS AND SMOKERS, July 1983, p. 3.
140 Telephone conversation, Jan. 7, 1985.
141 WALL STREET JOURNAL, "Many Burned-Up Bosses," op. cit.
142 NONSMOKERS AND SMOKERS, March 1982, p. 7.
143 Telephone conversation, Nov. 4, 1984.
144 See Note 35. Also: N. Collishaw and L. Mulligan, "Recent Trends in Tobacco Consumption in Canada and Other Countries," op. cit., pp. 52-4.
145 "Attitudes of the Public," op. cit., pp. 302-10.
146 Ibid., p. 307.
147 Ibid., p. 309.
148 See Note 4.
149 See Note 40.
150 "Tobacco Smoke, Ventilation and Indoor Air Quality," op. cit., p. 903.
151 WORKLIFE Magazine.
152 WALL STREET JOURNAL, "Many Burned-Up Bosses," op. cit.
153 Telephone conversation with Gaston Ruel, company buyer, Feb. 8, 1985.
154 Sep. 23, 1975, p. 1.
155 William Weis, "Can You Afford to Hire Smokers?" PERSONNEL ADMINISTRATOR, May 1981, pp. 71-8.
       Also: William Weis, "The Smoke-Free Workplace: Cost and Health Consequences," presented to the Fifth World Conference on Smoking and Health, Winnipeg, July 1983.
156 BUSINESS 1980 (Published by the Dartnell Corporation).
157 Canadian Press report, Oct. 7, 1984.
158 Ibid.
159 THE GLOBE AND MAIL [Toronto], July 12, 1983.
160 THE POLITICS OF CANCER, Sierra Club Books (San Francisco 1978) p. 470.
161 Canadian Medical Association statement. See Note 26.